DESIGNER
GREETING CARDS

Rockport Publishers, Rockport, Massachusetts

First published in the United States of America by:
Rockport Publishers, Inc.
146 Granite Street
Rockport, Massachusetts 01966
Telephone: (508) 546-9590
Fax: (508) 546-7141

Distributed to the book trade and art trade in the U.S. and Canada by:
North Light, an imprint of
F & W Publications
1507 Dana Avenue
Cincinnati, Ohio 45207
Telephone: (513) 531-2222

Other Distribution by:
Rockport Publishers, Inc.
Rockport, Massachusetts 01966

ISBN 1-56496-081-1

10 9 8 7 6 5 4 3 2

Art Direction and Cover Design: Laura P. Herrmann
Designer: Beth Santos Design
Production Manager: Barbara States
Production Assistant: Pat O'Maley
Cover Photograph: Benoit Photography, Gloucester, MA

Printed in Hong Kong

TABLE OF CONTENTS

INTRODUCTION

For centuries,  society has acknowledged special occasions by sending written greet- ings. Ancient Romans had messengers deliver to friends and family New Years' salutations that were inscribed on terra-cotta tablets. As technology progressed, so did all forms of invitations, announcements, and greeting cards. By the late nineteenth century, announcements and invitations were extremely popular and elaborate. Victorian society's respect for social decorum elevated the greeting card to "high art." Three-dimensional "pop-up" greetings and handmade cards were decorated with frilly embellishments of lace and ribbon.

During the twentieth century, sophisticated design and illustration tech- niques, as well as the advent of offset lithography, have resulted in the mass- prod- uction of printed cards and announcements. Well-wishers stopped making their own cards, preferring the eye-catching and colorful professional results obtained from their local lithographer and the ease and convenience of purchasing them at a local card shop.

When typesetting became computerized in the 70s, graphic designers—previously relegated only to advertising, packaging, and publication design—were increasingly employed to design the printed invitations and announcements that had formerly been the exclusive domain of printers and engravers. In  their hands, these written messages truly became designer greetings.

The business community also became savvy to the marketing impact of a promotional message packaged in the guise of a well-designed announcement or greeting card. For example, an eye-catching invitation when might recruit more attendees for fundraising events. As copywriters and graphic designers were hired to collaborate on these pieces, the line between social and business announcements and greetings and direct mail marketing started to blur. Invitations to special events became sophisticated, multicomponent mailers using clever folds and die-cuts. Moving announcements came packaged with a celebratory bottle of champagne, custom-labeled and incorporated into a coordinated promotional package. Seasonal greetings came in the form of a holiday recipe book, wall calendar, or poster.

Those in the business of designing print promotion have done their part to contribute to the evolution of the greeting card. For years, advertising agencies and graphic design studios have jumped at the chance to promote their creative services with a provocative holiday card or invitation to an open house. One has only to look at invitations to events held by design and advertising clubs to witness cutting-edge design.

In fact, many graphic designers feel their finest work is often reflected in the design of a personal greeting card, invitation, or announcement. Artistic freedom comes when designers are unleashed from client-imposed restrictions. Creative and individual expression merge, particularly when the special event or holiday has personal significance. The result is a printed piece that stretches well beyond the ordinary—expressing a designers' personality as well as showcasing his or her design unique ability.

This collection of graphic designers' invitations, announcements, and greeting cards represents some of the most cleverly conceived and beautifully designed work to be found anywhere. The scope and variety of artistic styles in this book not only reflects state-of-the-art design for greeting cards, it also celebrates creative expression.

— Poppy Evans

Poppy Evans is a graphic designer and author of many books and articles on the graphic arts. She teaches graphic design and computer publishing at the college level.

left
DESIGN FIRM SIEBERT DESIGN ASSOCIATES
ART DIRECTOR LORI SIEBERT
DESIGNER DAVID CARROLL
OCCASION SHOW OPENING
ILLUSTRATOR DAVID CARROLL, SUSAN NAYLOR
CLIENT ENSEMBLE THEATRE OF CINCINNATI

top
DESIGN FIRM SHIMOKOCHI/REEVES
ART DIRECTOR MAMORU SHIMOKOCHI,
  ANNE REEVES
DESIGNER MAMORU SHIMOKOCHI,
  TRACY MCGOLDRICK
OCCASION OPEN HOUSE FOR NEW OFFICE
CLIENT SHIMOKOCHI/REEVES

We're Saving A place for you!

We're Moving our Celebration from place to place. Colorado was the place of the marriage of our daughter Jocelyn to Steve Sacks. Des Moines is the place where we're saving a place for you. The place to be!

DESIGN FIRM SAYLES GRAPHIC DESIGN
ART DIRECTOR JOHN SAYLES
DESIGNER JOHN SAYLES
OCCASION WEDDING
ILLUSTRATOR JOHN SAYLES
CLIENT THE BLUMENTHAL FAMILY

top
DESIGN FIRM SAYLES GRAPHIC DESIGN
ART DIRECTOR JOHN SAYLES
DESIGNER JOHN SAYLES
OCCASION FAMILY REUNION
CLIENT THE ANDERSON FAMILY
EACH OF THE ATTENDEES RECEIVED A HANDMADE
BOX WHICH INCLUDED AN ITINERARY, VINTAGE
FAMILY PHOTO, AND THE RECOLLECTIONS AND
STORIES OF ANCESTORS.

bottom
DESIGN FIRM JEFF REYNOLDS DESIGN
ART DIRECTOR JEFF REYNOLDS
DESIGNER JEFF REYNOLDS
OCCASION BIRTHDAY PARTY
PHOTOGRAPHER EVANS STUDIO
CLIENT JEFF REYNOLDS

so they call their families from the Virgin Islands to tell them that they got married and so her mother cries and his family wasn't home so he leaves messages for everyone but his brother thought he was in jail down in Mexico when he got the message and calls back the next morning and he gives his sister the wrong phone number so she's calling this laundromat on some island somewhere but they finally got it all cleared up and they had a great vacation except for the plane ride home which took twelve hours but it was ok because they they did elope, and so all along they had planned this celebration with their family and friends with this cool steel drum band and some really tasty food made by her friend the famous caterer, which is neat, and all these interesting people will come to this place in the woods just north of Chitown, which is neat because it's nature and laid back and the Earth Day thing and so that's the whole reason for this story.

above
DESIGN FIRM MARK OLDACH DESIGN
ART DIRECTOR MARK OLDACH
DESIGNER MARK OLDACH
OCCASION WEDDING INVITATION
ILLUSTRATOR MARK OLDACH
CLIENT MARK OLDACH, JANET LORAT

right
DESIGN FIRM SOMMESE DESIGN
ART DIRECTOR KRISTIN SOMMESE, LANNY SOMMESE
DESIGNER KRISTIN SOMMESE
OCCASION BIRTH ANNOUNCEMENT
ILLUSTRATOR LANNY SOMMESE
CLIENT SAIGE SOMMESE

MIRACLES CAN HAPPEN AND DREAMS DO COME TRUE.
ON JANUARY 18, 1994 LANNY AND KRISTIN SOMMESE
HAD AN 8 POUND BOUNCING BABY GIRL.
HER NAME IS SAIGE ELIZABETH BEAL AND SHE
ALREADY HAS MORE HAIR THAN HER DADDY.

top left
DESIGN FIRM SOMMESE DESIGN
ART DIRECTOR KRISTIN SOMMESE,
LANNY SOMMESE
DESIGNER KRISTIN SOMMESE
OCCASION WEDDING INVITATION
ILLUSTRATOR LANNY SOMMESE
CLIENT LANI & ANDRE LUTHARD

bottom left
DESIGN FIRM MICHAEL STANARD, INC.
ART DIRECTOR KRISTY ROBERTS,
TOM VANDEKERCKHOVE
DESIGNER KRISTY ROBERTS, TOM VANDEKERCKHOVE
OCCASION WEDDING INVITATION
CLIENT KRISTY ROBERTS, TOM VANDEKERCKHOVE

right
DESIGN FIRM LAUGHLIN/WINKLER INC.
ART DIRECTOR MARK LAUGHLIN, ELLEN WINKLER
DESIGNER MARK LAUGHLIN, ELLEN WINKLER
OCCASION WEDDING INVITATION
CLIENT MARK LE SAFFRE, AVERY SMITH

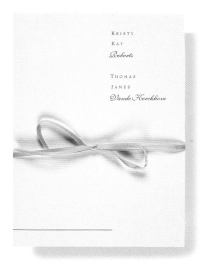

DESIGN FIRM SULLIVANPERKINS
ART DIRECTOR RON SULLIVAN
DESIGNER LINDA KELTON
OCCASION BIRTH ANNOUNCEMENT
ILLUSTRATOR LINDA KELTON
CLIENT DUFFY WEIR

DESIGN FIRM SULLIVANPERKINS
ART DIRECTOR ART GARCIA
DESIGNER ART GARCIA
OCCASION BIRTH ANNOUNCEMENT
PHOTOGRAPHER GERRY KANO
CLIENT PRESCOTT FAMILY

On March 4th
Dan and Stephanie
learned they
had E.S.P.

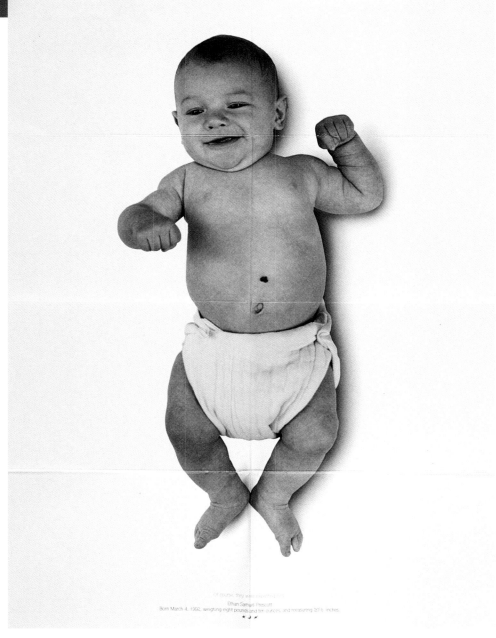

Ethan Samuel Prescott
Born March 4, 1992, weighing eight pounds and ten ounces, and measuring 20⅞ inches.

We always
wondered if we
were cut out
to be parents.

Kira Christine Mires Born on October 29, 1990, at 5:06 pm, to parents Lori and Scott. Weight, 6 pounds; length, 18 inches and an absolute living doll.

top
DESIGN FIRM MIRES DESIGN, INC.
ART DIRECTOR SCOTT MIRES
DESIGNER SCOTT MIRES
OCCASION BIRTH ANNOUNCEMENT
PHOTOGRAPHER CHRIS WIMPEY
CLIENT SCOTT AND LORI MIRES

bottom
DESIGN FIRM THE DYNAMIC DUO, INC.
ART DIRECTOR ARLEN SCHUMER
DESIGNER ARLEN SCHUMER
OCCASION BIRTH OF 1ST CHILD
ILLUSTRATOR THE DYNAMIC DUO, INC.

Robin
and Gwen
Breslin
are proud
to announce
the completion
of their new
addition...

DESIGN FIRM SOMMESE DESIGN
ART DIRECTOR KRISTIN SOMMESE, LANNY SOMME
DESIGNER KRISTIN SOMMESE
OCCASION BIRTH ANNOUNCEMENT
ILLUSTRATOR LANNY SOMMESE
CLIENT ROBIN & GWEN BRESLIN
IMAGE WAS SELECTED BECAUSE BOTH PARENTS ARE
ARCHITECTS.

We've Added a New Lim to Our Family Tree

Kenneth "Justin" Lim
7 lbs. 3 oz.
19.75 inches long
Born: August 12, 1993
to Randy & Elana Lim

left
DESIGN FIRM STUDIO MD
ART DIRECTOR RANDY LIM, JESSE DOQUILO,
GLENN MITSUI
DESIGNER RANDY LIM
OCCASION BIRTH ANNOUNCEMENT
PHOTOGRAPHER RANDY LIM
CLIENT RANDY, ELANA & JUSTIN LIM
MATERIALS FOR THIS PIECE INCLUDE TWIGS, BARK
PAPER, AND RECYCLED PAPER.

right
DESIGN FIRM HORNALL ANDERSON DESIGN
WORKS
ART DIRECTOR JACK ANDERSON
DESIGNER JACK ANDERSON, LEO RAYMUNDO
OCCASION BIRTH ANNOUNCEMENT
CLIENT STEVE SHAHBAGHLIAN, TISH OYE

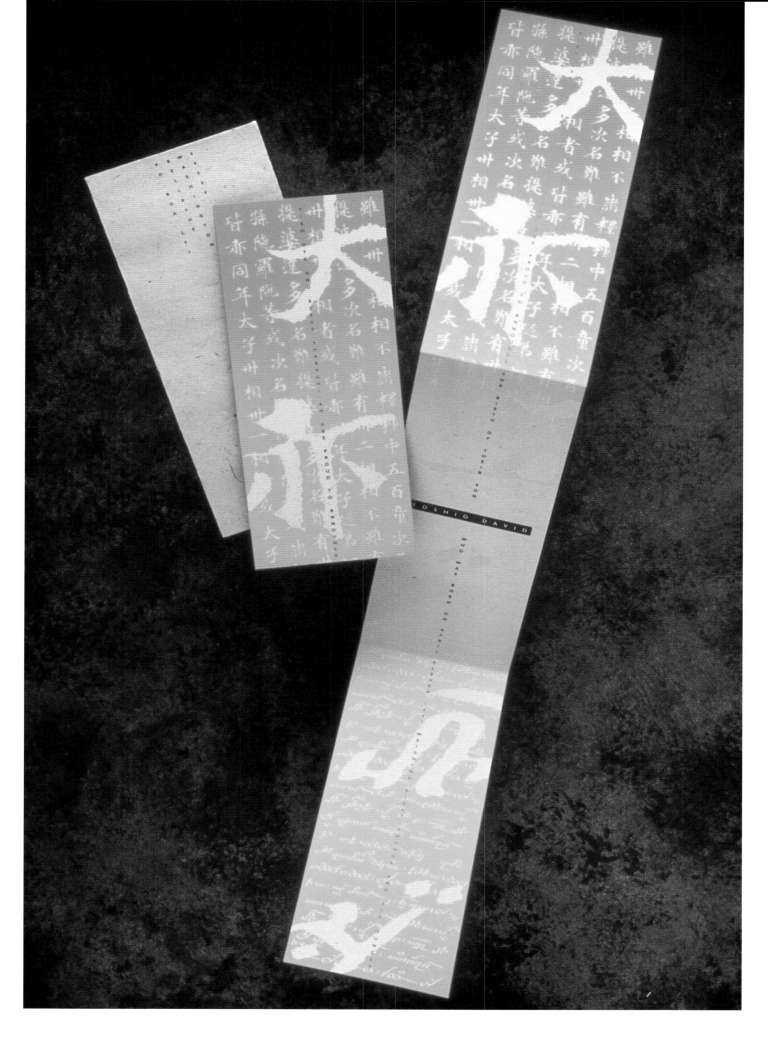

left
DESIGN FIRM SOMMESE DESIGN
ART DIRECTOR KRISTIN SOMMESE,
LANNY SOMMESE
DESIGNER KRISTIN SOMMESE
OCCASION WEDDING INVITATION
ILLUSTRATOR LANNY SOMMESE
CLIENT LANNY AND KRISTIN SOMMESE

right top
DESIGN FIRM MODERN DOG
ART DIRECTOR TOM & MARY
DESIGNER ROBYNNE RAYE
OCCASION WEDDING INVITATION
ILLUSTRATOR ROBYNNE RAYE,
MICHAEL STRASSBURGER
CLIENT TOM & MARY
EACH INTED WAS MAILED WITH A STICK OF GUM.

right bottom
DESIGN FIRM MICHAEL STANARD, INC.
ART DIRECTOR LISA FINGERHUT
DESIGNER KRISTY ROBERTS
OCCASION WEDDING INVITATION
CLIENT JENNIFER KUNETKA

Mary Louise Ransom
and
Thomas Matthew Allen
Together with their Parents
Anne and Ed Ransom
Sharon Allen and Richard Allen
Invite you to celebrate the
happiness and fun of their marriage.
12:00 Noon Saturday October 16, 1993
Saint Therese Catholic Church
Seattle, Washington
Reception to Follow at Leschi Lake Cafe

Map Enclo

top
DESIGN FIRM SHIMOKOCHI/REEVES
ART DIRECTOR MAMORU SHIMOKOCHI,
ANNE REEVES
DESIGNER MAMORU SHIMOKOCHI,
ANNE REEVES
OCCASION MOVING ANNOUNCEMENT
CLIENT SHIMOKOCHI/REEVES

bottom
DESIGN FIRM SULLIVANPERKINS
ART DIRECTOR RON SULLIVAN
DESIGNER DARREL KOLOSTA
OCCASION OPEN HOUSE INVITATION
ILLUSTRATOR DARREL KOLOSTA
CLIENT ARTESIAN PRESS

top
Design Firm SullivanPerkins
Art Director Art Garcia
Designer Art Garcia
Occasion Moving Announcement
Illustrator Art Garcia
Client Wolf Family

bottom
Design Firm Mires Design, Inc.
Art Director Scott Mires
Designer Scott Mires
Occasion Moving Announcement
Photographer Chris Wimpey
Client Mires Design, Inc.

TO THE OPENING
OF A NEW OFFICE EXPERIENCE
ONE CAMPUS VIEW

Penco Development Co., the Pontifical College
Josephinum, and the retail merchants cordially invite
you to be their guest at the Open House Celebration
of One Campus View, a luxury
office and retail project is located at the entrance of
Crosswoods Center, just north of Worthington,
Route 23 or I-270. Please join them Wednesday,
September 10, 1986 from 4:30-7:30, for cocktails and
hors d'oeuvres. R.S.V.P by September 8th to Melanie
Circle, Vantage Companies 846-4900

OPEN · HERE

YOUR
PERSONAL
INVITATION

OPEN · HERE

DESIGN FIRM RICKABAUGH GRAPHICS
ART DIRECTOR ERIC RICKABAUGH
DESIGNER ERIC RICKABAUGH
OCCASION OPEN HOUSE
PHOTOGRAPHER TOM WATSON
CLIENT VANTAGE COMPANIES

top
Design Firm Siebert Design Associates
Art Director Lori Siebert
Designer Lori Siebert
Occasion Family Day Museum Opening
Illustrator Lori Siebert
Client Cincinnati Art Museum

bottom
Design Firm WS Design
Art Director Wayne Sakamoto
Designer Wayne Sakamoto
Occasion Re-Opening Celebration
Client Tamalpais Dog Grooming

First • Paper
Second • Cotton
Third • Leather
Fourth • Linen
Fifth • Wood
Sixth • Iron
Seventh • Wool or copper
Eighth • Bronze
Ninth • Pottery
Tenth • Tin
Eleventh • Steel
Twelfth • Silk
Thirteenth • Lace
Fourteenth • Ivory
Fifteenth • Crystal
Twentieth • China
Twenty-fifth • Jade
Fortieth • Rubies
Fiftieth • Gold
Fifty-fifth • Emeralds
Sixtieth • Diamonds
Seventy-fifth • Diamonds

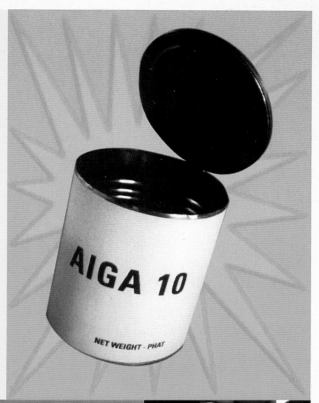

top
DESIGN FIRM FARENHEIT
ART DIRECTOR CAROLYN MONTIE, PAUL MONTIE
DESIGNER PAUL MONTIE, CAROLYN MONTIE
OCCASION A.I.G.A./BOSTON 10TH
  ANNIVERSARY BASH
PHOTOGRAPHER KENT DAYTON
CLIENT A.I.G.A./BOSTON

bottom
DESIGN FIRM SAYLES GRAPHIC DESIGN
ART DIRECTOR JOHN SAYLES
DESIGNER JOHN SAYLES
OCCASION RESTAURANT GRAND OPENING
ILLUSTRATOR JOHN SAYLES
CLIENT NACHO MAMMAS

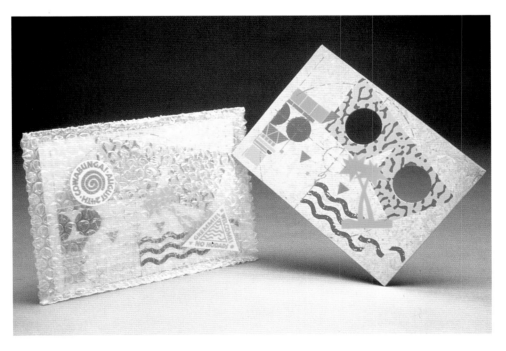

top
DESIGN FIRM NEW IDEA DESIGN, INC.
DESIGNER RON BOLDT
OCCASION MOVING ANNOUNCEMENT
ILLUSTRATOR RON BOLDT
CLIENT WESTERN PAPER COMPANY

bottom
DESIGN FIRM HORNALL ANDERSON DESIGN
  WORKS
ART DIRECTOR JOHN HORNALL,
  JACK ANDERSON
DESIGNER JOHN HORNALL, JACK ANDERSON,
  JULIE TANAGI-LOCK
OCCASION MOVING/OPEN HOUSE
  ANNOUNCEMENT
CLIENT HORNALL ANDERSON DESIGN WORKS

BIG DEALS

BIG DAY. Thursday, November 5, during this year's ICSC Deal Making Convention in Dallas, Gary Shafer and the retail partners of Trammell Crow Company invite you to a special after-hours party. It's a great way to end a big day.

BIG TIME. That evening from 7:30 P.M. to 10:30 P.M. we'll host a buffet and cocktails. Transportation to the party will be provided from the Anatole Hotel, Chantilly Entrance, at 7:15, 7:30 and 7:45 P.M., with return service every fifteen minutes. So make plans to have a great time with us.

DESIGN FIRM SULLIVANPERKINS
ART DIRECTOR RON SULLIVAN
DESIGNER MICHAEL SPRONG
OCCASION BUILDING OPENING
ILLUSTRATOR MICHAEL SPRONG
CLIENT TRAMMEL CROW COMPANY

Over the years, all the gifts of the magic Queen were enchanted with Peace And Harmony.

♥

our team glad to invite you to the **Grand Opening** of

EIKON CREATIONS

Date : 23rd October 1993 Saturday
Time : 10:00a.m. - 5:00p.m.
Address : 919 Metro Centre, 21 Lam Hing St.
Kowloon Bay, Kowloon, Hong Kong.
Phone : 852.7560213 Fax : 852.7591020

Once upon a time there lived a magician

DESIGN FIRM EIKON CREATIONS
ART DIRECTOR HEIDE KWOK
DESIGNER TOMMY WONG, KENNETH CHOI
OCCASION GRAND OPENING
ILLUSTRATOR PEOPLE HO
CLIENT EIKON CREATIONS

San Antonio's brightest Star is brighter than ever.

left
DESIGN FIRM SULLIVANPERKINS
ART DIRECTOR RON SULLIVAN
DESIGNER LINDA KELTON
OCCASION SHOPPING CENTER RE-OPENING
INVITE
CLIENT THE ROUSE COMPANY/NORTHSTAR
SHOPPING CENTER

right
DESIGN FIRM MODERN DOG
ART DIRECTOR MICHAEL STRASSBURGER
DESIGNER MICHAEL STRASSBURGER
OCCASION MODERN DOG OPEN HOUSE
CLIENT MODERN DOG

You are invited!

Is Having a Party!
April 5, 1994
6:30pm

601 Valley Street #309
Seattle, Wa. 98109
Tel: (206) AT2-8857 Fx: 281-8293

The party is in our studio which is on the southeast corner of 6th and Valley, two blocks northeast from the downtown Tower Redords, and one block west of Aurora in a plain brick building on the top floor. Good luck finding us!

top
Design Firm Rickabaugh Graphics
Art Director Eric Rickabaugh
Designer Eric Rickabaugh
Occasion Open House
Photographer Tony Stone (Stock)
Client Thomas W. Ruff

bottom
Design Firm Sayles Graphic Design
Art Director John Sayles
Designer John Sayles
Occasion Wedding Invitation
Illustrator John Sayles
Client Teri & Andy TeBockhorst

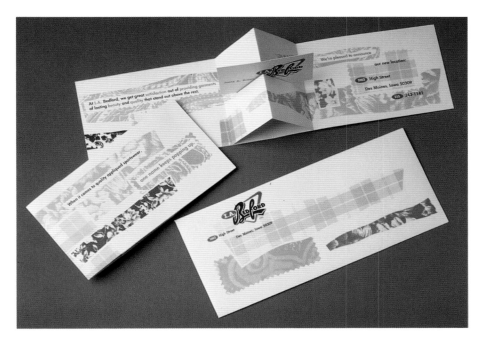

top
DESIGN FIRM THE DUNLAVEY STUDIO
ART DIRECTOR MICHAEL DUNLAVEY
DESIGNER LINDY DUNLAVEY
OCCASION OPENING PARTY INVITATION
CLIENT JAVA CITY AT MARKET SQUARE

bottom
DESIGN FIRM SAYLES GRAPHIC DESIGN
ART DIRECTOR JOHN SAYLES
DESIGNER JOHN SAYLES
OCCASION MOVING ANNOUNCEMENT
CLIENT I.A. BEDFORD

DESIGN FIRM INDEPENDENT PROJECT PRESS
ART DIRECTOR BRUCE & KAREN LICHER
DESIGNER BRUCE & KAREN LICHER
OCCASION FIRST ANNUAL EARTH SHOW
PHOTOGRAPHER BRUCE LICHER
CLIENT MERGING ONE GALLERY

Design Firm Rickabaugh Graphics
Art Director Eric Rickabaugh
Designer Eric Rickabaugh
Occasion Printer's Open House
  Invitation
Illustrator Eric Rickabaugh
Client Byrum Lithographics

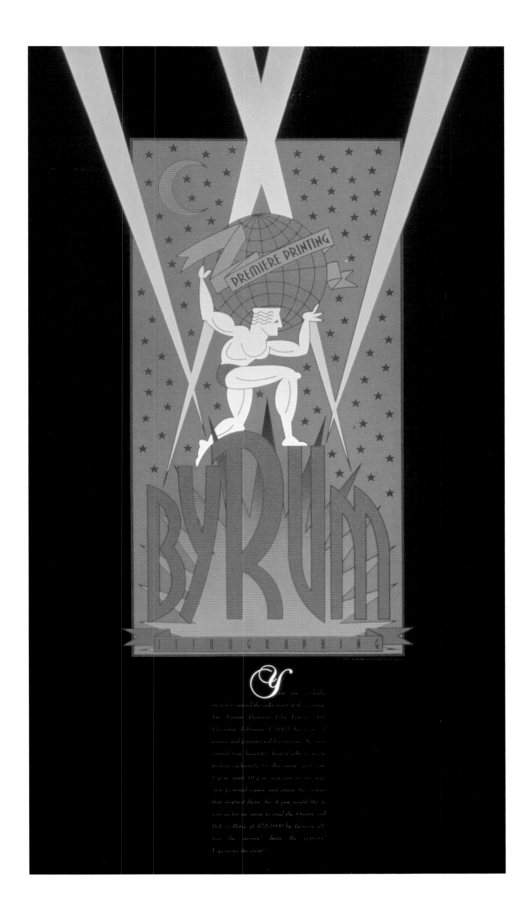

DESIGN FIRM M/W DESIGN
ART DIRECTOR ALLISON MUENCH,
  J.P. WILLIAMS
OCCASION OPENING ANNOUNCEMENT
CLIENT TAKASHIMAYA NEW YORK

DESIGN FIRM STUDIO MD
ART DIRECTOR JESSE DOQUILO, RANDY LIM,
  GLENN MITSUI
DESIGNER JESSE DOQUILO
OCCASION MOVING ANNOUNCEMENT
PHOTOGRAPHER JESSE DOQUILO
ILLUSTRATOR JESSE DOQUILO
CLIENT STUDIO MD

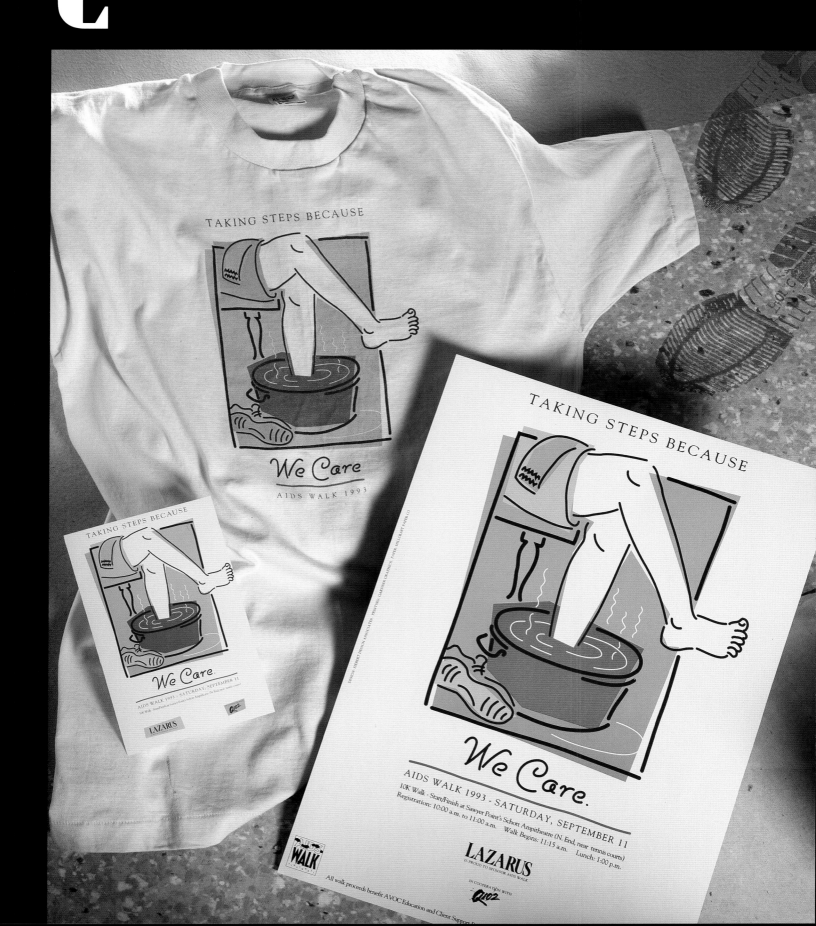

far left
DESIGN FIRM SIEBERT DESIGN ASSOCIATES
ART DIRECTOR LORI SIEBERT
DESIGNER LISA BALLARD
OCCASION FUNDRAISING WALK
ILLUSTRATOR LISA BALLARD, DAVID CARROLL
CLIENT AIDS WALK

top
DESIGN FIRM JOHN BRADY DESIGN CONSULTANTS
ART DIRECTOR JOHN BRADY
DESIGNER TERRI SEWALD
OCCASION EXECUTIVE CONFERENCE
CLIENT GSI

left
DESIGN FIRM SAYLES GRAPHIC DESIGN
ART DIRECTOR JOHN SAYLES
DESIGNER JOHN SAYLES
OCCASION VENDOR WELCOME KIT
ILLUSTRATOR JOHN SAYLES
CLIENT TEAM UNIX

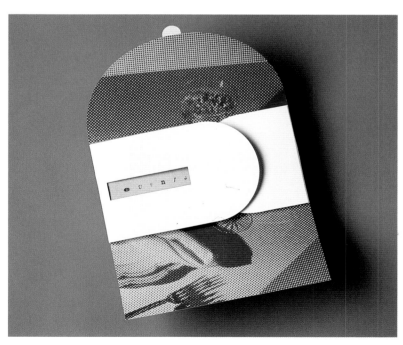

far left
DESIGN FIRM CHARLES S. ANDERSON DESIGN CO.
ART DIRECTOR CHARLES S. ANDERSON
DESIGNER CHARLES S. ANDERSON, DANIEL OLSON
OCCASION TOKYO EXHIBITION
ILLUSTRATOR CHARLES S. ANDERSON, DANIEL
OLSON, RANDALL DAHLK
CLIENT GINZA GRAPHIC GALLERY

bottom left
DESIGN FIRM CHARLES S. ANDERSON DESIGN CO.
ART DIRECTOR CHARLES S. ANDERSON
DESIGNER CHARLES S. ANDERSON
OCCASION TOKYO EXHIBIT
PHOTOGRAPHER PAUL IRMITER
CLIENT GINZA GRAPHIC GALLERY

left and top
DESIGN FIRM MULLER + COMPANY
ART DIRECTOR JOHN MULLER
DESIGNER PETER CORCORAN
PHOTOGRAPHER PETER CORCORAN
CLIENT KANSAS CITY ART INSTITUTE

DESIGN FIRM THE DYNAMIC DUO, INC.
ART DIRECTOR ARLEN SCHUMER
DESIGNER ARLEN SCHUMER
OCCASION NEW YORK ART DIRECTORS
  CLUB LECTURE
CLIENT THE DYNAMIC DUO, INC.

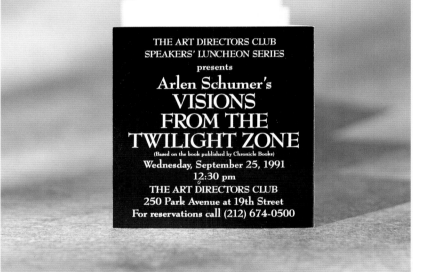

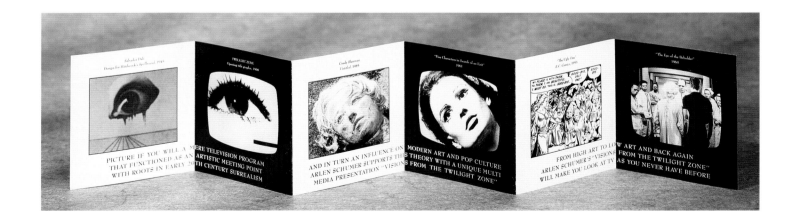

CHARLES S. ANDERSON

NEW MEMBERS...Martha Bogdanoff (Bozell, Inc.), Mary Brandt (Laser Tech Color, Inc.), Ron Head, Tina Kuntz (Harwood Marketing Group), Doug Smith (Doug Smith Photography), Carl Waters (Univ. of Texas Southwestern Medical Center).

DALLAS TEXAS
THURSDAY OCT. 24TH AT CITY PLACE
MEMBERS
FREE
COCKTAILS 6:00 PM SPEAKER 7:00
CHUCK WAGON LANTERN
non-members $10 students $3 Call 241-2017

Litho Inc
Printing a
St. Paul, M

FRENCH PAI
SPONSOR

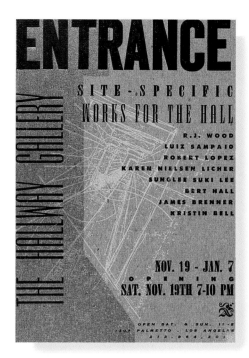

ENTRANCE
THE HALLWAY GALLERY
SITE-SPECIFIC
WORKS FOR THE HALL
R.J. WOOD
LUIZ SAMPAIO
ROBERT LOPEZ
KAREN NIELSEN LICHER
SUNGLEE SUKI LEE
BERT HALL
JAMES BRENNER
KRISTIN BELL
NOV. 19 - JAN. 7
OPENING
SAT. NOV. 19TH 7-10 PM

top left
DESIGN FIRM CHARLES S. ANDERSON DESIGN CO.
ART DIRECTOR CHARLES S. ANDERSON
DESIGNER CHARLES S. ANDERSON
OCCASION LECTURE
CLIENT DALLAS SOCIETY OF VISUAL COMMUNICATION

top right
DESIGN FIRM INDEPENDENT PROJECT PRESS
ART DIRECTOR BRUCE LICHER
DESIGNER BRUCE LICHER
OCCASION BRUCE LICHER EXHIBITION
CLIENT THE HALLWAY GALLERY

bottom
DESIGN FIRM MIRES DESIGN, INC.
ART DIRECTOR JOHN BALL
DESIGNER JOHN BALL
OCCASION OFFICERS' ELECTION
ILLUSTRATOR DAVID QUATTROCIOCHI
CLIENT COMMUNICATING ARTS GROUP

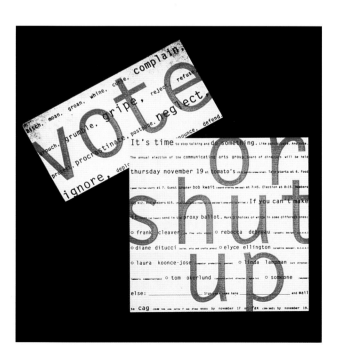

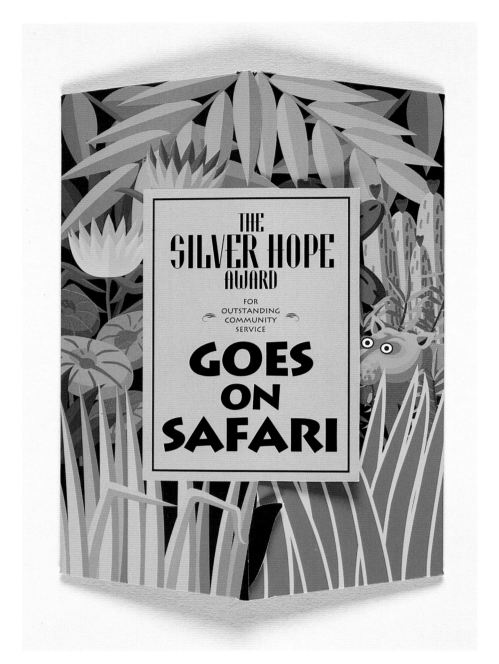

DESIGN FIRM JEFF REYNOLDS DESIGN
ART DIRECTOR JEFF REYNOLDS
DESIGNER JEFF REYNOLDS
OCCASION ANNUAL FUNDRAISING BANQUET
ILLUSTRATOR JEFF REYNOLDS
CLIENT MULTIPLE SCLEROSIS SOCIETY

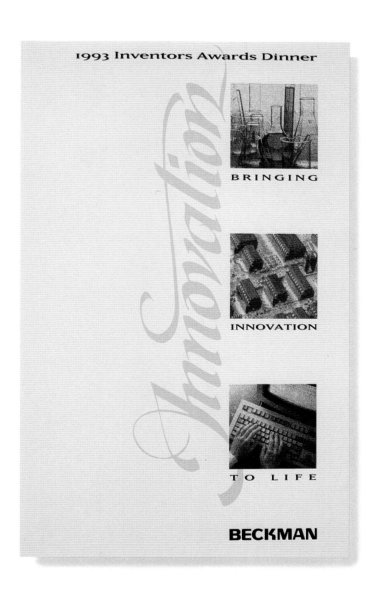

1993 Inventors Awards Dinner

BRINGING

INNOVATION

TO LIFE

BECKMAN

Ed Metzger as "Albert Einstein"

Performing vignettes from his one-man show "Albert Einstein: The Practical Bohemian" is actor, writer Ed Metzger. Ed has had an expansive career in films, television, and the Broadway stage. He successfully brought "Einstein" to the stage in 1978 at The Matrix Theater in Los Angeles. The following year, Ed performed his "Einstein" in New York's Off-Broadway. Since then Ed has performed at major theaters throughout the country including The John F. Kennedy Center for The Performing Arts in Washington, D.C.

DESIGN FIRM BECKMAN CORPORATE GRAPHICS CENTER
ART DIRECTOR PATRICIA HUIZAR
DESIGNER MIKA TOYOURA
OCCASION INVENTOR AWARDS DINNER
CALLIGRAPHY BONNIE LEAH
CLIENT BECKMAN INSTRUMENTS, INC., LEGAL DEPARTMENT, V.P. GENERAL COUNSEL

top left
DESIGN FIRM STUDIO MD
ART DIRECTOR CAROL PHILLIPS,
MARITZ PERFORMANCE IMPROVEMENT CO.
DESIGNER JESSE DOQUILO, STUDIO MD
OCCASION NISSAN DEALER
ANNOUNCEMENT SHOW
ILLUSTRATOR JESSE DOQUILO
CLIENT NISSAN

bottom left
DESIGN FIRM SULLIVANPERKINS
ART DIRECTOR RON SULLIVAN
DESIGNER JON FLAMING
OCCASION MERCHANTS RENOVATION
ANNOUNCEMENT
ILLUSTRATOR JON FLAMING
CLIENT TOPANGA PLAZA/CENTERMARK
DEVELOPMENT

right
DESIGN FIRM SIEBERT DESIGN ASSOCIATES
ART DIRECTOR LORI SIEBERT
DESIGNER LORI SIEBERT, JEFF FASSNACHT
OCCASION FUNDRAISER
ILLUSTRATOR JOHN PATRICK
CLIENT SCHOOL FOR CREATIVE & PERFORMING
ARTS

ral Trust and the School for Creative and Performing Arts present
Tickets 632-5910
Nov.
0-29
OLiVeR!
The Taft The
The 19
SCPA
ordially Invite
THE FRIENDS OF THE SCHOOL FOR CREATIVE AND PERFORMING ARTS
1310 Sycamore Street
Cincinnati, Ohio 45210
NON-PROFIT ORG. U.S. POSTAGE PAID PERMIT NO. 4398 CINCINNATI, OHIO
Gala Committee Members
The SCPA production of "Oliver!" is sponsored by Central Trust
5:30 p.m.
"Consider Yourself" part of the London scene, enjoying cocktails and hors d'oeuvres while surrounded by strolling musicians.
6:45 p.m.
Feast on "Food, Glorious Food" (no gruel here!) at a sumptuous four course dinner, while overlooking the "London Bridge."
8:30 p.m.
As "Big Ben" chimes, the curtain will rise on the SCPA
Gala
Atruim II
221 East Fourth Street
OLiVeR! with a Twist
honors SCPA's own Dianne Dunkelman.
"She'd Do Anything" for us and we consider ourselves lucky that she's "Part of the Family."
Taft Theatre
Production
5th & Sycamore

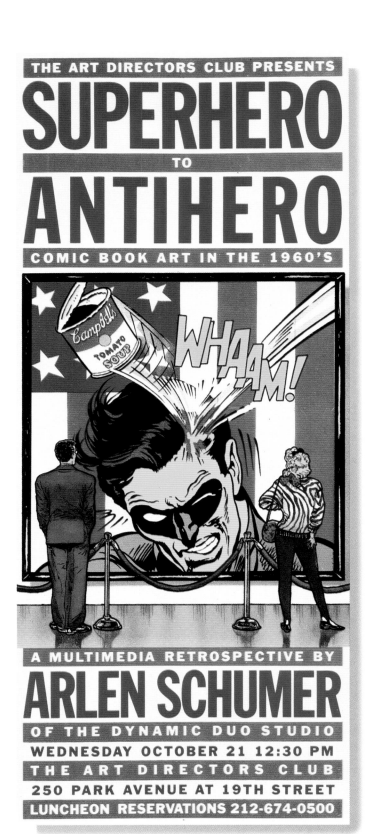

DISCOVER JAPAN

All Nippon Airways 1994 Summer Program in Japan

An adventure of a lifetime awaits you. Five DC area students will be chosen to spend the summer of '94 with Japanese host families. Contact your guidance counselor today for an application or Youth For Understanding at 1-800-673-2728. Students must have a C average or better and demonstrate general suitability for a cross-cultural living experience. The ANA Summer Program in Japan is administered by YFU International Exchange.

ANA
All Nippon Airways
Japan's best to the world.

far left
DESIGN FIRM THE DYNAMIC DUO, INC.
ART DIRECTOR ARLEN SCHUMER
DESIGNER ARLENE SCHUMER
OCCASION MULTI-PROJECTOR SLIDE
  SHOW/LECTURE AT THE NEW YORK ART
  DIRECTORS CLUB
ILLUSTRATOR THE DYNAMIC DUO, INC.
DESIGN & LINE ART ARLEN SCHUMER
COLOR SHERRI WOLFGANG
CLIENT SELF PROMOTIONAL
GREEN LANTERN © D.C. COMICS 1970

left
DESIGN FIRM SUPON DESIGN GROUP, INC.
ART DIRECTOR ANDREW DOLAN,
  SUPON PHORNIRUNLIT
DESIGNER ANDREW DOLAN
OCCASION ANNOUNCEMENT FOR JAPAN TRIP
ILLUSTRATOR ANDREW DOLAN
CLIENT ALL NIPPON AIRWAYS

above
DESIGN FIRM SIEBERT DESIGN ASSOCIATES
ART DIRECTOR LORI SIEBERT
DESIGNER DIANE SULLIVAN
OCCASION FUNDRAISER
ILLUSTRATOR VARIOUS
CLIENT CONTEMPORARY ARTS CENTER

T : DESIGNER CARD 48-49

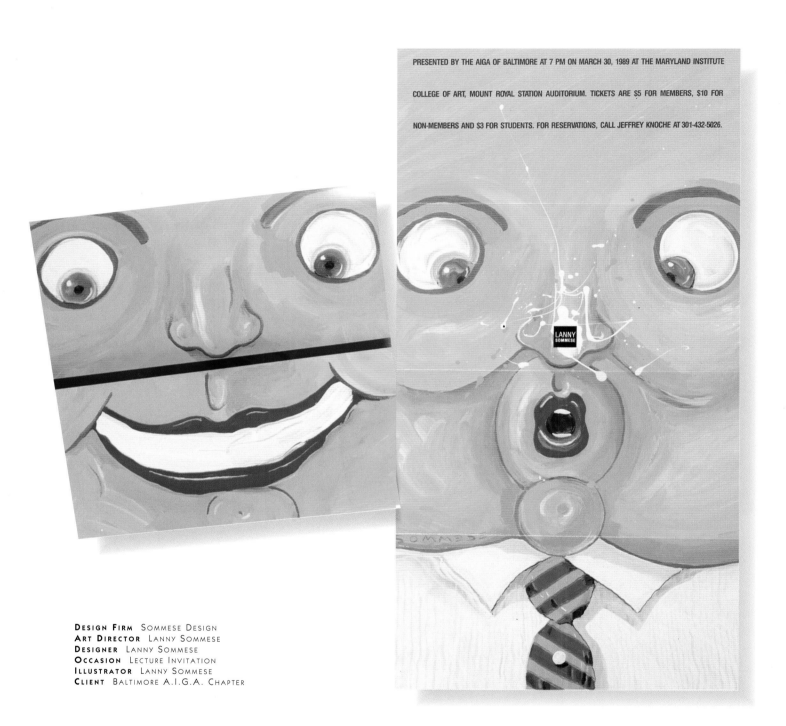

PRESENTED BY THE AIGA OF BALTIMORE AT 7 PM ON MARCH 30, 1989 AT THE MARYLAND INSTITUTE COLLEGE OF ART, MOUNT ROYAL STATION AUDITORIUM. TICKETS ARE $5 FOR MEMBERS, $10 FOR NON-MEMBERS AND $3 FOR STUDENTS. FOR RESERVATIONS, CALL JEFFREY KNOCHE AT 301-432-5026.

Design Firm Sommese Design
Art Director Lanny Sommese
Designer Lanny Sommese
Occasion Lecture Invitation
Illustrator Lanny Sommese
Client Baltimore A.I.G.A. Chapter

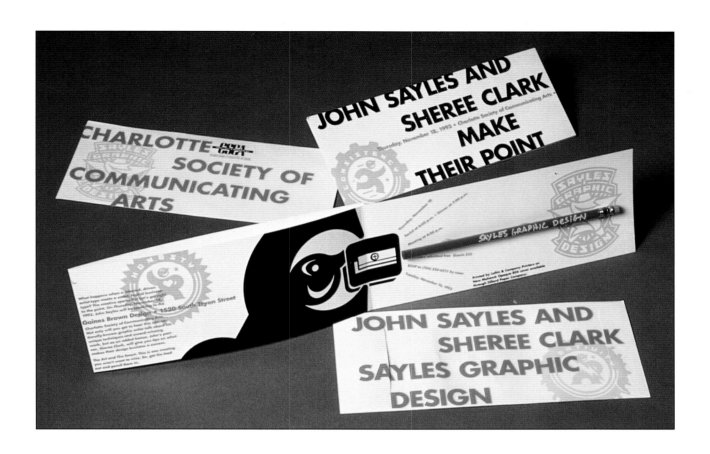

above
DESIGN FIRM SAYLES GRAPHIC DESIGN
ART DIRECTOR JOHN SAYLES
DESIGNER JOHN SAYLES
OCCASION JOHN SAYLES AND SHEREE CLARK
  MAKE THEIR POINT
ILLUSTRATOR JOHN SAYLES
CLIENT CHARLOTTE SOCIETY OF
  COMMUNICATING ARTS

right
DESIGN FIRM SOMMESE DESIGN
ART DIRECTOR LANNY SOMMESE
DESIGNER LANNY SOMMESE
OCCASION LECTURE
ILLUSTRATOR LANNY SOMMESE
CLIENT A.I.G.A. OMAHA

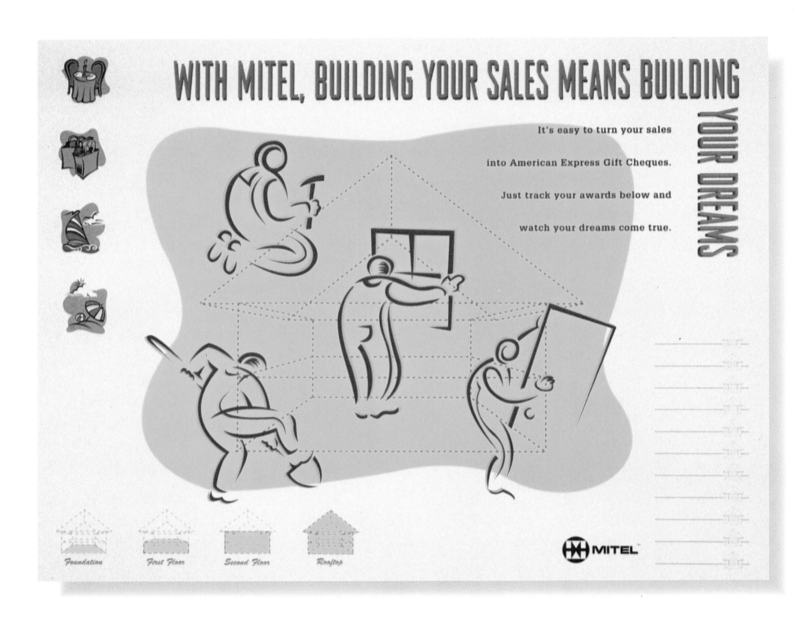

WITH MITEL, BUILDING YOUR SALES MEANS BUILDING

YOUR DREAMS

It's easy to turn your sales

into American Express Gift Cheques.

Just track your awards below and

watch your dreams come true.

Foundation   First Floor   Second Floor   Rooftop

MITEL

Amazing! MODERN COMMERCIAL! New IDEAS

VISUAL ARTS MUSEUM NEW YORK NY
C.S. ANDERSON DESIGN WORKS

OPENING RECEPTION: Wednesday, March 21, 6-8 pm SLIDE LECTURE: Tues., March 20, 10:45am-12:00 SVA Theater, Visual Arts Museum 209 East 23rd Street, New York City, 10010, Phone: (212) 679-7350

left top
DESIGN FIRM SUPON DESIGN GROUP, INC.
ART DIRECTOR SUPON PHORNIRUNLIT
DESIGNER RICHARD BOYNTON
OCCASION ANNOUNCEMENT FOR SALES CAMPAIGN
ILLUSTRATOR ANDREW DOLAN
CLIENT MITEL, INC.

left bottom
DESIGN FIRM CHARLES S. ANDERSON DESIGN CO.
ART DIRECTOR CHARLES S. ANDERSON
DESIGNER DANIEL OLSON, CHARLES S. ANDERSON
OCCASION EXHIBITION
ILLUSTRATOR RANDALL DAHLK
CLIENT VISUAL ARTS MUSEUM

right
DESIGN FIRM CHARLES S. ANDERSON DESIGN CO.
ART DIRECTOR CHARLES S. ANDERSON
DESIGNER CHARLES S. ANDERSON,
  TODD HAUSWIRTH
OCCASION LECTURE
COPY LISA PEMRICK
CLIENT ART DIRECTORS ASSOCIATION OF
  DES MOINES, IOWA

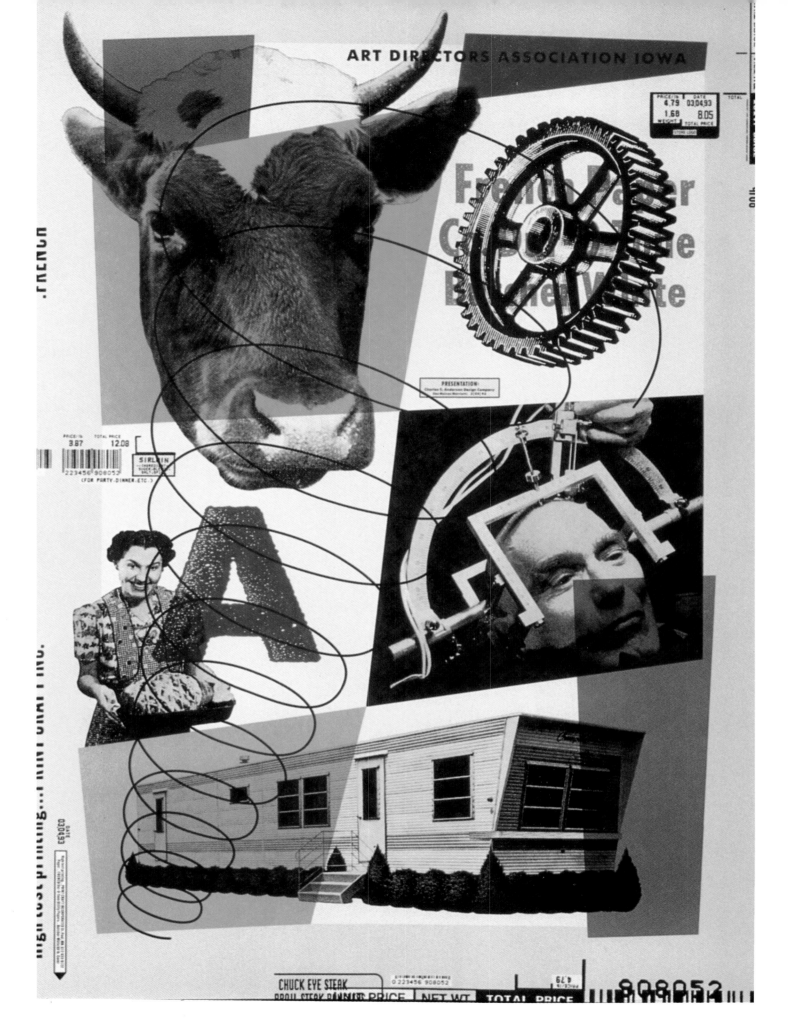

ART DIRECTORS ASSOCIATION IOWA

DESIGN FIRM MIRES DESIGN, INC.
ART DIRECTOR JÓSE SERRANO
DESIGNER JÓSE SERRANO
OCCASION POSTCARDS
PHOTOGRAPHER VARIOUS STOCK PHOTOS
CLIENT DELEO CLAY TILE COMPANY

top
DESIGN FIRM John Brady Design Consultants
ART DIRECTOR John Brady
DESIGNER Joseph Tomko
OCCASION Designer Dialogue Series
PHOTOGRAPHER Christopher Caffee
CLIENT AIGA/Pittsburgh

bottom
DESIGN FIRM Michael Stanard, Inc.
ART DIRECTOR Michael Stanard, Inc.
DESIGNER Marcos Chavez
OCCASION AIGA Show
CLIENT AIGA

DESIGN FIRM MODERN DOG
ART DIRECTOR JERI HEIDEN
DESIGNER MICHAEL STRASSBURGER
OCCASION GRAMMY CONGRATULATIONS CARD
ILLUSTRATOR MICHAEL STRASSBURGER
CLIENT WARNER BROTHERS RECORDS

Congratulations to All of Our 1993 Grammy Winners!

Eric Clapton
Unplugged (6 Grammy Awards!)
Miles Davis • *Doo-Bop*
Enya • *Shepherd Moons*
*Handel's Messiah –
A Soulful Celebration*
**Emmylou Harris &
The Nash Ramblers**
Live At The Ryman
Al Jarreau • *Heaven And Earth*
Dr. John
Goin' Back To New Orleans
Chaka Khan • *The Woman I Am*
k.d. lang • *Ingénue*
Red Hot Chili Peppers
BloodSugarSexMagik
Sir Mix-A-Lot • *Mack Daddy*
Travis Tritt
It's All About To Change

Warner Bros. and Reprise Records

And to Their Labels:
Warner Bros. • **Reprise** • **Sire** •
Def American • **Duck** • **Rhyme Cartel**

It's your memory. It's our history. It's worth saving.

PRESERVATION WEEK • MAY 8-14, 1994 • NATIONAL TRUST FOR HISTORIC PRESERVATION

top
DESIGN FIRM SUPON DESIGN GROUP, INC.
ART DIRECTOR ANDREW DOLAN,
   SUPON PHORNIRUNLIT
DESIGNER ANDREW DOLAN
OCCASION ANNOUNCEMENT FOR
   PRESERVATION WEEK
ILLUSTRATOR ANDREW DOLAN
CLIENT NATIONAL TRUST FOR HISTORIC
   PRESERVATION

bottom
DESIGN FIRM SOMMESE DESIGN
ART DIRECTOR LANNY SOMMESE, KRISTIN SOMMESE
DESIGNER KRISTIN SOMMESE
OCCASION HALLOWEEN COSTUME BLACK TIE BALL
   FUNDRAISER
ILLUSTRATOR LANNY SOMMESE
CLIENT CINQUENTA WOMENS CLUB

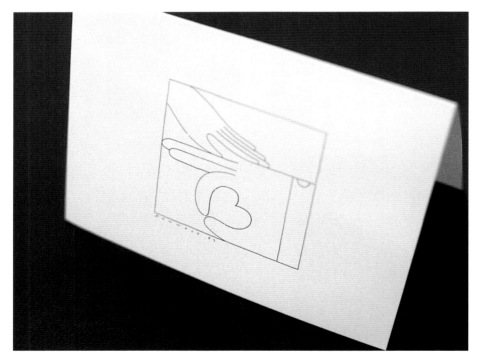

top
DESIGN FIRM MICHAEL STANARD, INC.
ART DIRECTOR MICHAEL STANARD, INC.
DESIGNER MARCOS CHAVEZ
OCCASION BUSINESS ANNOUNCEMENT
CLIENT DOUGLAS STANARD

bottom
DESIGN FIRM SOMMESE DESIGN
ART DIRECTOR A.I.G.A. PITTSBURGH
OCCASION VALENTINE, "ART FROM THE HEART
 FUNDRAISER"
ILLUSTRATOR LANNY SOMMESE
CLIENT A.I.G.A. PITTSBURGH

top
DESIGN FIRM MIRES DESIGN, INC.
OCCASION FUNDRAISER FOR VICTIMS OF
CROATIAN WAR
ILLUSTRATOR GERALD BUSTAMANTE
CLIENT ANUSKA SMITH

bottom
DESIGN FIRM RICKABAUGH GRAPHICS
ART DIRECTOR ERIC RICKABAUGH, MARK
KRUMEL
DESIGNER MARK KRUMEL
OCCASION FUNDRAISING EVENT
PHOTOGRAPHER LARRY HAMILL
ILLUSTRATOR TONY MEUSER
CLIENT ALZHEIMER'S FOUNDATION

DESIGN FIRM SIEBERT DESIGN ASSOCIATES
ART DIRECTOR LORI SIEBERT
DESIGNER LORI SIEBERT, BARB RAYMOND
OCCASION TRADE SHOW EXHIBIT
ILLUSTRATOR LORI SIEBERT
CLIENT HEWLETT PACKARD

THE AMERICAN CRAFT MUSEUM CORDIALLY INVITES YOU TO

frank

American Craft Museum
40 West 53rd Street
New York, New York 10019

DESIGN FIRM PLATINUM DESIGN, INC.
ART DIRECTOR V. PESLAK
DESIGNER K. SCHUMACHER
OCCASION PARTY INVITATION
CLIENT AMERICAN CRAFT MUSEUM

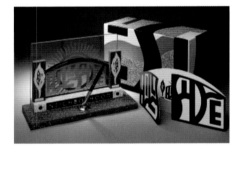

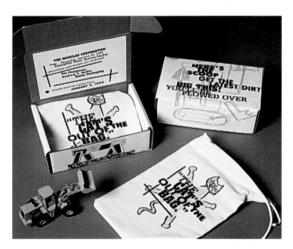

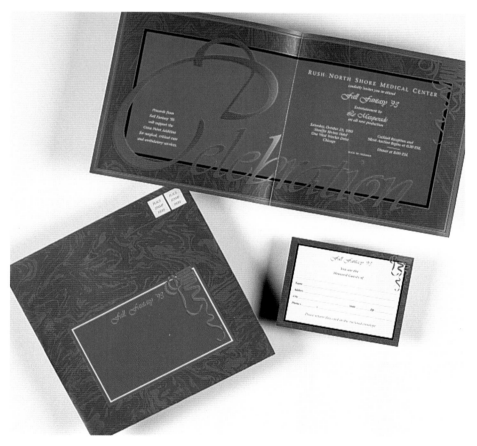

opposite top
DESIGN FIRM SAYLES GRAPHIC DESIGN
ART DIRECTOR JOHN SAYLES
DESIGNER JOHN SAYLES
OCCASION BOYS & GIRLS CLUB FUNDRAISER
ILLUSTRATOR JOHN SAYLES
CLIENT BOYS & GIRLS CLUB

opposite center left
DESIGN FIRM SAYLES GRAPHIC DESIGN
ART DIRECTOR JOHN SAYLES
DESIGNER JOHN SAYLES
OCCASION FUNDRAISING/GOLF EVENT
ILLUSTRATOR JOHN SAYLES
CLIENT SCIENCE CENTER OF IOWA

opposite center
DESIGN FIRM SAYLES GRAPHIC DESIGN
ART DIRECTOR JOHN SAYLES
DESIGNER JOHN SAYLES
OCCASION SEMINAR INVITATION
ILLUSTRATOR JOHN SAYLES
CLIENT IOWA TREASURY MANAGEMENT
ASSOCIATION

opposite center right
DESIGN FIRM SAYLES GRAPHIC DESIGN
ART DIRECTOR JOHN SAYLES
DESIGNER JOHN SAYLES
OCCASION NEW PLANNED LIVING COMMUNITY
ANNOUNCEMENT
ILLUSTRATOR JOHN SAYLES
CLIENT HILLSIDE NEIGHBORHOOD

opposite bottom
DESIGN FIRM SAYLES GRAPHIC DESIGN
ART DIRECTOR JOHN SAYLES
DESIGNER JOHN SAYLES
OCCASION "THE CAT'S OUT OF THE BAG"
ILLUSTRATOR JOHN SAYLES
CLIENT YOUNG PRESIDENTS ORGANIZATION

left
DESIGN FIRM WATTS DESIGN, INC.
ART DIRECTOR ED WATTS
DESIGNER ED WATTS
OCCASION "FALL FANTASY" HOSPITAL BENEFIT
CLIENT RUSH NORTH SHORE MEDICAL CENTER

left top
DESIGN FIRM SAYLES GRAPHIC DESIGN
ART DIRECTOR JOHN SAYLES
DESIGNER JOHN SAYLES
OCCASION EMPLOYEE ANNOUNCEMENT
ILLUSTRATOR JOHN SAYLES
CLIENT VERMEER MANUFACTURING

left bottom
DESIGN FIRM SAYLES GRAPHIC DESIGN
ART DIRECTOR JOHN SAYLES
DESIGNER JOHN SAYLES
OCCASION AWARD ANNOUNCEMENT
ILLUSTRATOR JOHN SAYLES
CLIENT SAYLES GRAPHIC DESIGN
AFTER "SWEEPING" THE ADDY AWARDS SHOW
FOR THE FIFTH CONSECUTIVE YEAR, SAYLES SENT
A DUSTPAN ANNOUNCEMENT TO CLIENTS.

right
DESIGN FIRM JOHN BRADY DESIGN
  CONSULTANTS
ART DIRECTOR JOHN BRADY
DESIGNER TERRI SEWALD
OCCASION EXECUTIVE CONFERENCE
CLIENT GSI

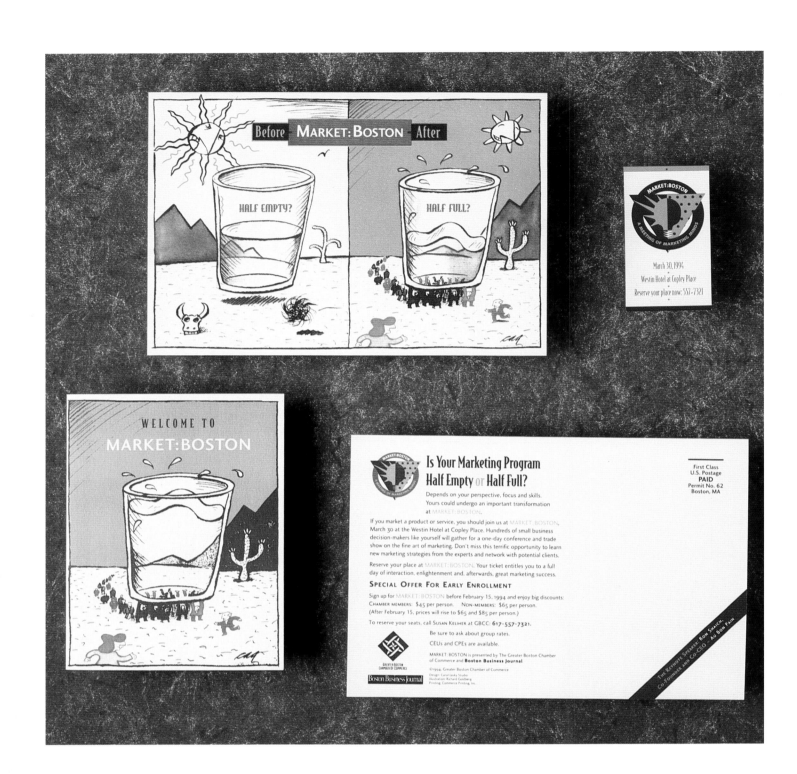

DESIGN FIRM CAROL LASKY STUDIO
CREATIVE DIRECTOR CAROL LASKY
LOGO DESIGNER LAURA HERRMANN
INVITATION DESIGNER ERIN DONNELLAN
OCCASION MARKETING EXHIBITION AND
 CONFERENCE "MARKET BOSTON"
ILLUSTRATOR RICHARD A. GOLDBERG
CLIENT GREATER BOSTON CHAMBER OF
 COMMERCE AND BOSTON BUSINESS JOURNAL

CORPORATE

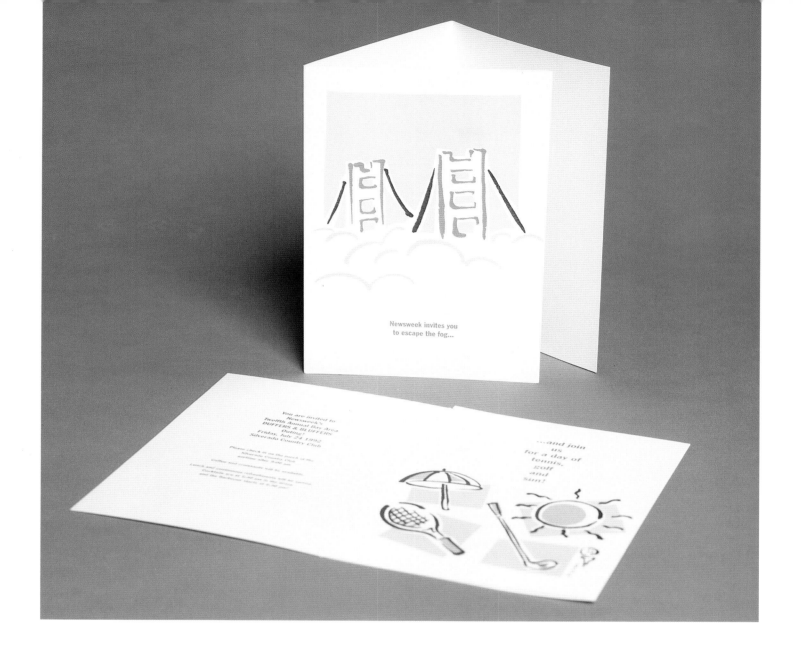

Newsweek invites you
to escape the fog...

You are invited to
Newsweek's
Twelfth Annual Bay Area
DUFFERS & BLUFFERS
Outing!
Friday, July 24 1992
Silverado Country Club

...and join
us
for a day of
tennis,
golf
and
sun!

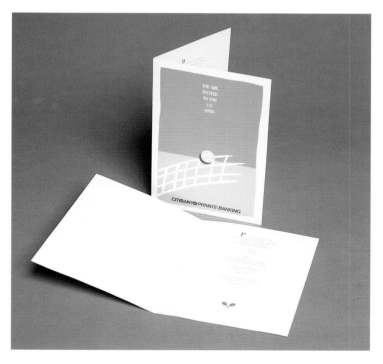

YOU ARE
INVITED
TO THE
U.S.
OPEN

CITIBANK PRIVATE BANKING

top
DESIGN FIRM MIKE QUON DESIGN OFFICE
ART DIRECTOR TRACY STARS
DESIGNER MIKE QUON
OCCASION SAN FRANCISCO CONFERENCE
ILLUSTRATOR MIKE QUON
CLIENT NEWSWEEK

bottom
DESIGN FIRM MIKE QUON DESIGN OFFICE
ART DIRECTOR MIKE QUON
DESIGNER MIKE QUON
OCCASION US OPEN INVITATION
ILLUSTRATOR MIKE QUON
CLIENT CITIBANK

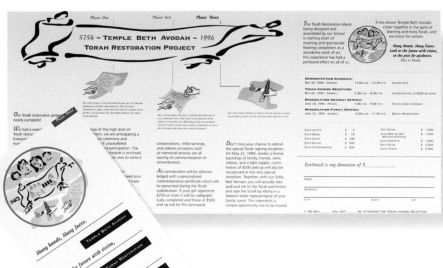

top
DESIGN FIRM MODERN DOG
ART DIRECTOR VITTORIO COSTARELLA,
   ROBYNNE RAYE
DESIGNER VITTORIO COSTARELLA
OCCASION NEW SNOWBOARD MODEL
   INVITATION
ILLUSTRATOR VITTORIO COSTARELLA
CLIENT K2 SNOWBOARDS

bottom
DESIGN FIRM BETH SANTOS DESIGN
ART DIRECTOR DAVE FRANK
DESIGNER BETH SANTOS
OCCASION TORAH RESTORATION FUNDRAISER
ILLUSTRATOR BETH SANTOS
CLIENT DIMENSIONAL RESPONSE

top
DESIGN FIRM SAYLES GRAPHIC DESIGN
ART DIRECTOR JOHN SAYLES
DESIGNER JOHN SAYLES
OCCASION "GREAT DESIGN TAKES CENTER STAGE"
ILLUSTRATOR JOHN SAYLES
CLIENT JAMES RIVER PAPER

bottom
DESIGN FIRM SAYLES GRAPHIC DESIGN
ART DIRECTOR JOHN SAYLES
DESIGNER JOHN SAYLES
OCCASION LECTURE ANNOUNCEMENT
ILLUSTRATOR JOHN SAYLES
CLIENT WOMEN IN COMMUNICATIONS, INC.

DESIGN FIRM LOVE PACKAGING GROUP
ART DIRECTOR TRACY HOLDEMAN
DESIGNER TRACY HOLDEMAN
OCCASION WICHITA JAZZ FESTIVAL/TRACY
   HOLDEMAN PROMOTION JAZZ FESTIVAL
   POSTER
PHOTOGRAPHER ROCK ISLAND STUDIOS
ILLUSTRATOR TRACY HOLDEMAN
CLIENT WICHITA JAZZ FESTIVAL, LOVE
   PACKAGING GROUP

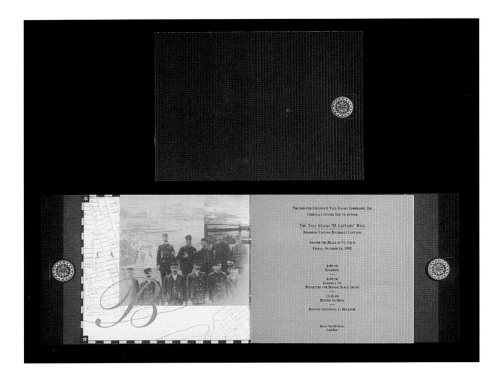

DESIGN FIRM KOLAR DESIGN, INC.
DESIGNER KELLY KOLAR, DEBORAH VATTER,
VICKY ZWISSLER
OCCASION THE TALL STACKS CAPTAINS BALL
PHOTOGRAPHER CINCINNATI HISTORICAL
SOCIETY ELDER PHOTOGRAPHIC, INC./INLAND
RIVERS LIBRARY
CLIENT GREATER CINCINNATI TALL STACKS
COMMISSION, INC.

DESIGN FIRM HORNALL ANDERSON DESIGN
  WORKS
ART DIRECTOR JACK ANDERSON
DESIGNER JACK ANDERSON, JANI DREWFS,
  LIAN NG
OCCASION PACIFIC NORTHWEST BALLET
  NUTCRACKER BALL
ILLUSTRATOR NANCY GELLOS
CLIENT PACIFIC NORTHWEST BALLET

INNOVATION

... It's that little twist— a little unexpected, sometimes surprising.

It's solving a small problem with ingenuity and flair.

It's solving a complex problem with insight and resourcefulness.

At Richard Yates Architects, we understand the importance of a fresh and creative approach.

Because the path to a solution is often filled with interesting turns.

Richard Yates Architects, Inc.

428 Sandoval
Santa Fe
New Mexico 87501
505/982-1913

INVITATION

... It is our expressed wish for you to join in the fun and celebration of our new location.

An invitation to view our most recent accomplishment—

the design and renovation of the place we now call home.

Be our guest for an afternoon of spirits and hors d'oeuvres.

Friday, September 26, 1986
1:00pm–5:00pm

Richard Yates Architects, Inc.

428 Sandoval
Santa Fe
New Mexico 87501
505/982-1913

top
DESIGN FIRM VAUGHN WEDEEN CREATIVE
ART DIRECTOR RICK VAUGHN
DESIGNER RICK VAUGHN
OCCASION OPEN HOUSE
CLIENT YATES ARCHITECTS

bottom
DESIGN FIRM MAMMOLITI CHAN DESIGN
ART DIRECTOR TONY MAMMOLITI
DESIGNER TONY MAMMOLITI, CHWEE KUAN CHAN
OCCASION AMBIENT ECLIPSE SEATING LAUNCH
ILLUSTRATOR TONY MAMMOLITI, CHWEE KUAN CHAN
CLIENT AMBIENT CONTRACT INTERIORS PTY. LTD.

DESIGN FIRM VAUGHN WEDEEN CREATIVE
ART DIRECTOR STEVE WEDEEN
DESIGNER STEVE WEDEEN
OCCASION NMBA CONVENTION
ILLUSTRATOR MARK CHAMBERLAIN
CLIENT NM BANKERS ASSOCIATION

DESIGN FIRM JOHN BRADY DESIGN CONSULTANTS
ART DIRECTOR MONA MACDONALD
DESIGNER RICK MADISON, MARK MURPHY
OCCASION GOURMET GALA
ILLUSTRATOR DAVID BOWERS
CLIENT MARCH OF DIMES

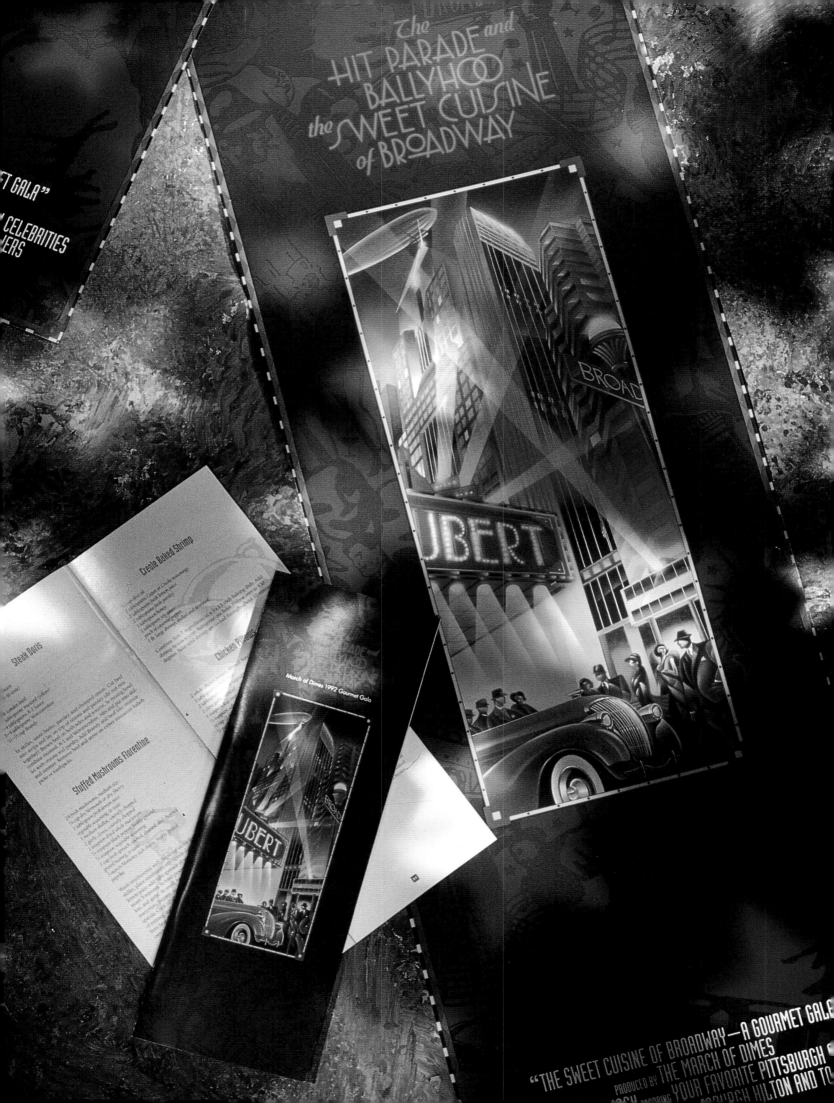

top
DESIGN FIRM MIRES DESIGN, INC.
ART DIRECTOR JÓSE SERRANO
DESIGNER JÓSE SERRANO
OCCASION ROWING REGATTA ANNOUNCEMENT
ILLUSTRATOR TRACY SABIN
CLIENT PENINSULA

bottom
DESIGN FIRM MIRES DESIGN, INC.
ART DIRECTOR JÓSE SERRANO
DESIGNER JOSE SERRANO
OCCASION ROWING REGATTA
ILLUSTRATOR GERALD BUSTAMANTE
CLIENT PENINSULA FAMILY YMCA

DESIGN FIRM MIRES DESIGN, INC.
ART DIRECTOR JÓSE SERRANO
DESIGNER JÓSE SERRANO
OCCASION ROWING REGATTA
ILLUSTRATOR GERALD BUSTAMANTE
CLIENT PENINSULA FAMILY YMCA

top
DESIGN FIRM PLATINUM DESIGN, INC.
ART DIRECTOR V. PESLAK
DESIGNER JOHN STAATS
OCCASION BENEFIT
CLIENT AMERICAN CRAFT

bottom
DESIGN FIRM MICHAEL STANARD, INC.
ART DIRECTOR MICHAEL STANARD
DESIGNER DAWN GOLDAMMER
OCCASION ORCHARD VILLAGE ANNIVERSARY
CELEBRATION
CLIENT ORCHARD VILLAGE

right
DESIGN FIRM SUPON DESIGN GROUP, INC.
ART DIRECTOR SUPON PHORNIRUNLIT
DESIGNER RICHARD LEE HEFFNER
OCCASION ANNOUNCEMENT FOR NATIONAL
ESSAY CONTEST
ILLUSTRATOR RICHARD LEE HEFFNER
CLIENT UNITED STATES INSTITUTE OF PEACE

NATIONAL PEACE ESSAY CONTEST 1993-1994

HIGH SCHOOL STUDENTS, GRADES 9-12
WIN UP TO $10,000 IN COLLEGE SCHOLARSHIPS!
WIN AN EXPENSE-PAID TRIP TO WASHINGTON, D.C.!
DEADLINE IS FEBRUARY 1, 1994

FOR THE 1993–94 TOPIC, CONTEST

GUIDELINES AND YEARBOOK, SEE

_____

CONTEST COORDINATOR, IN

_____

NATIONAL PEACE ESSAY CONTEST UNITED STATES INSTITUTE OF PEACE
1550 M STREET, NW   SUITE 700   WASHINGTON, DC 20005-1708

♻ Printed on recycled paper.

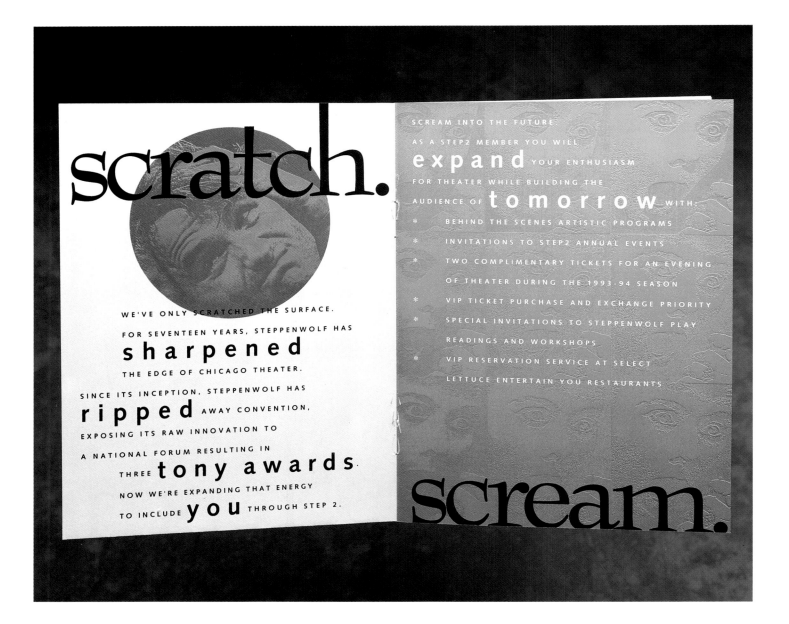

scratch.

WE'VE ONLY SCRATCHED THE SURFACE.

FOR SEVENTEEN YEARS, STEPPENWOLF HAS
sharpened
THE EDGE OF CHICAGO THEATER.

SINCE ITS INCEPTION, STEPPENWOLF HAS
ripped AWAY CONVENTION,
EXPOSING ITS RAW INNOVATION TO

A NATIONAL FORUM RESULTING IN
THREE **tony awards**.
NOW WE'RE EXPANDING THAT ENERGY
TO INCLUDE **you** THROUGH STEP 2.

SCREAM INTO THE FUTURE.
AS A STEP2 MEMBER YOU WILL
expand YOUR ENTHUSIASM
FOR THEATER WHILE BUILDING THE
AUDIENCE OF **tomorrow** WITH:

* BEHIND THE SCENES ARTISTIC PROGRAMS
* INVITATIONS TO STEP2 ANNUAL EVENTS
* TWO COMPLIMENTARY TICKETS FOR AN EVENING
  OF THEATER DURING THE 1993-94 SEASON
* VIP TICKET PURCHASE AND EXCHANGE PRIORITY
* SPECIAL INVITATIONS TO STEPPENWOLF PLAY
  READINGS AND WORKSHOPS
* VIP RESERVATION SERVICE AT SELECT
  LETTUCE ENTERTAIN YOU RESTAURANTS

scream.

DESIGN FIRM MARK OLDACH DESIGN
ART DIRECTOR MARK OLDACH
DESIGNER MARK OLDACH
OCCASION STEP 2 MEMBERSHIP INVITE
CLIENT STEPPENWOLF THEATRE

TAKE A BITE...

OF THE ENERGY AND CREATIVITY BREWING AT

steppenwolf

THEATRE COMPANY

STEPPENWOLF THEATRE CELEBRATES THE KICK OFF

OF **step2** ON JULY 16, 1993.

STEP2 IS A DYNAMIC NEW GROUP

FOR THE YOUNG AND **innovative**

WITH A CURIOSITY AND DESIRE

TO TASTE THE

spirit

OF EVOCATIVE THEATER.

bite.

step²

kick.

1993

Dear Friend of Northlight Theatre,

By definition, North means "situated toward or at the north."
Light is defined as "stimulating vision, enlightening, informative" and Theatre is
"a forum for artistic expression through live performance."

A Friend is described as "one attached to another by affection" and "one who favors
or promotes something." By subscribing to Northlight, you have demonstrated your support
and affection for a theatre that stimulates vision, enlightens, and informs.

As a not-for-profit theatre, Northlight relies on contributions to fulfill
the 40% of the operating budget not covered by ticket sales. We hope that you will show an
additional commitment to Northlight by making a donation to our eighteenth season.

Without the generosity of individuals like you, Northlight Theatre
would not be possible. Our future is your gift.

With every good wish,

Russell Vandenbroucke
RUSSELL VANDENBROUCKE
ARTISTIC DIRECTOR, NORTHLIGHT THEATRE

DESIGN FIRM MICHAEL STANARD, INC.
ART DIRECTOR MICHAEL STANARD, INC.
DESIGNER MARC FUHRMAN
OCCASION ANNUAL GALA EVENT
CLIENT NORTHLIGHT THEATRE

Is It Fate—If a funny, energetic, perceptive, compassionate Jewish male (I forgot, handsome) of 31, met an upbeat, personable, cute, kind Jewish female who can enjoy a burger at "White Castle" as much as a stroll on white sands, as long as she's happy? NYM R655

...th like sensibilities. Seek... ...Photo. NYM R654

CELEBRATE FATE!

DESIGN FIRM PLATINUM DESIGN, INC.
ART DIRECTOR S. QUINN, V. PESLAK
DESIGNER S. QUINN
OCCASION PARTY
CLIENT AMERICAN CRAFT MUSEUM

EVENTS

top
DESIGN FIRM S&N DESIGN
ART DIRECTOR STEVE LEE
DESIGNER STEVE LEE
OCCASION "OKLAHOMA" PERFORMANCE
ILLUSTRATOR STEVE LEE
CLIENT MCCAIN AUDITORIUM

bottom
DESIGN FIRM THE DUNLAVEY STUDIO, INC.
ART DIRECTOR MICHAEL DUNLAVEY
DESIGNER LINDY DUNLAVEY
OCCASION "AMAZING BUT TRUE" 50' PARTY
  INVITATION
CLIENT THE DUNLAVEY STUDIO, INC.

top
DESIGN FIRM RICKABAUGH GRAPHICS
ART DIRECTOR ERIC RICKABAUGH
DESIGNER TINA ZIENTARSKI
OCCASION THANK YOU PARTY
ILLUSTRATOR MIKE SMITH
CLIENT GRANT MEDICAL CENTER

bottom
DESIGN FIRM MAMMOLITI CHAN DESIGN
ART DIRECTOR TONY MAMMOLITI
DESIGNER CHWEE KUAN CHAN
OCCASION AMBIENT TRAFFIX SEATING LAUNCH
CLIENT AMBIENT CONTRACT INTERIORS PTY. LTD.
TRAFFIC LIGHTS WERE HAND COLORED BY STAFF
WITH MARKERS AND A RED LOLLIPOP WAS
ATTACHED TO INVITATION.

CALIFORNIA STYLE

YOU ARE INVITED

DESIGN FIRM PLATINUM DESIGN, INC.
ART DIRECTOR V. PESLAK, M. NORTON
DESIGNER M. NORTON
OCCASION PARTY
CLIENT OPTYL

OPTYL
invites you to
cocktails
to salute
CALIFORNIA STYLE
Friday
September 20th
6:30 p.m.
to 8:30 p.m.

Sunset Deck at
The Anaheim Hilton
777 Convention Way
5th Floor
Anaheim, California
R.S.V.P.
Loving & Weintraub
212-935-1033

CALIFORNIA STYLE

We're rounding up the Party Posse
for a Hoe-Down at the
AOPA PILOT Ranch and
we need a Marshall to lead it.
Oshkosh is comin' up and
we're gonna put on some barbecue,
draw down on some tall, cold ones
and dance up a storm.
So grab your buckaroo or buckarette
and wrangle on over.

AOPA PILOT RANCH
354 Legion Place, Oshkosh, WI
July 31, 1992
6:30 pm till the cows come home
Tell us if you're gonna saddle up by July 17
Mary "Two Guns" Roland   301-695-2053

AOPA PILOT

top
DESIGN FIRM BOELTS BROS. DESIGN, INC.
ART DIRECTOR ERIC BOELTS, JACKSON BOELTS, KERRY STRATFORD
DESIGNER ERIC BOELTS, JACKSON BOELTS, KERRY STRATFORD
OCCASION TRADESHOW PARTY
CLIENT AOPA PILOT

bottom
DESIGN FIRM RICKABAUGH GRAPHICS
ART DIRECTOR ERIC RICKABAUGH
DESIGNER TINA ZIENTARSKI
OCCASION WORLD SERIES PARTY
CLIENT MILLCRAFT PAPER COMPANY

DESIGN FIRM WCVB TV DESIGN
ART DIRECTOR MARC ENGLISH
DESIGNER MARC ENGLISH
OCCASION WCVB TV SALES PARTY
ILLUSTRATOR MARC ENGLISH
CLIENT WCVB TV BOSTON/SALES

DESIGN FIRM SAYLES GRAPHIC DESIGN
ART DIRECTOR JOHN SAYLES
DESIGNER JOHN SAYLES
OCCASION PARTY
CLIENT SAYLES GRAPHIC DESIGN

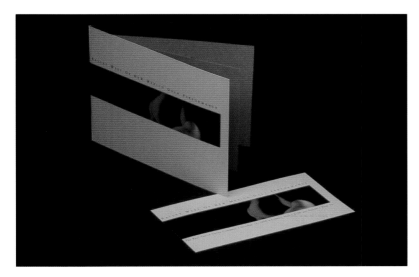

top
DESIGN FIRM VAUGHN WEDEEN CREATIVE
ART DIRECTOR RICK VAUGHN
DESIGNER RICK VAUGHN
OCCASION 10TH ANNIVERSARY PARTY
CLIENT VAUGHN WEDEEN CREATIVE

bottom
DESIGN FIRM VAUGHN WEDEEN CREATIVE
ART DIRECTOR STEVE WEDEEN
DESIGNER STEVE WEDEEN
OCCASION PAUL TAYLOR DANCE CO. GALA
  PERFORMANCE
PHOTOGRAPHER MICHAEL BARLEY
CLIENT BALLET WEST OF NEW MEXICO

HOLIDAY

THROUGH THE EYES OF CHILDREN WE CAN
SEE THE WAY TO BUILD A BETTER WORLD.

Lesley Kropidlowski, age 14

Michelle Crissip, age 12

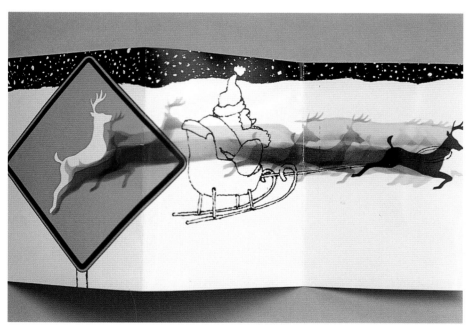

left
DESIGN FIRM MARK OLDACH DESIGN
ART DIRECTOR MARK OLDACH
DESIGNER DON EMERY
OCCASION CHRISTMAS CARD
CLIENT CATERPILLAR INC.

top
DESIGN FIRM CHERMAYEFF & GEISMAR, INC.
ART DIRECTOR STEFF GEISSBUHLER
DESIGNER STEFF GEISSBUHLER, LISETTE BUIANI
OCCASION HOLIDAY CARD
CLIENT ANCHOR ENGRAVING CO. AND FAMILY OF
    STEFF GEISSBUHLER
CLIENT SAYLES GRAPHIC DESIGN

bottom
DESIGN FIRM SOMMESE DESIGN
ART DIRECTOR LANNY SOMMESE
DESIGNER LANNY SOMMESE
OCCASION CHRISTMAS CARD
PHOTOGRAPHER LANNY SOMMESE
ILLUSTRATOR LANNY SOMMESE
CLIENT SOMMESE DESIGN

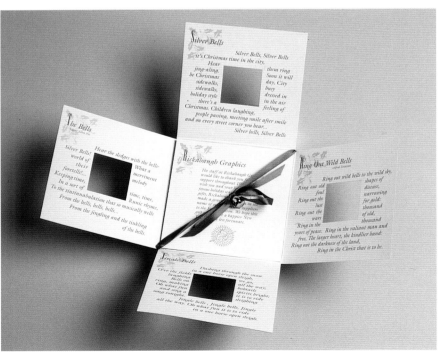

DESIGN FIRM RICKABAUGH GRAPHICS
ART DIRECTOR ERIC RICKABAUGH
DESIGNER TINA ZIENTARSKI
OCCASION CHRISTMAS CARD
CLIENT RICKABAUGH GRAPHICS

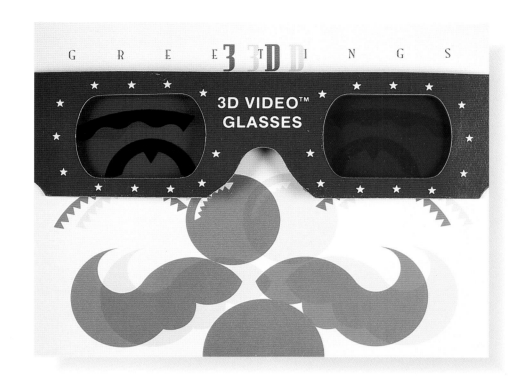

3D VIDEO™ GLASSES

top
DESIGN FIRM RICKABAUGH GRAPHICS
ART DIRECTOR ERIC RICKABAUGH
DESIGNER MARK KRUMEL
OCCASION CHRISTMAS CARD
ILLUSTRATOR TONY MEUSER
CLIENT RICKABAUGH GRAPHICS
CARD WAS ACCOMPANIED BY A PAIR OF 3D GLASSES.

left
DESIGN FIRM DESIGN HORIZONS INTERNATIONAL
ART DIRECTOR EILEEN NOREN
DESIGNER BRYAN SANZOTTI, KRISTA FERDINAND,
  JANAN CHIN, DEAN SPRAGUE
OCCASION HOLIDAY WRAPPING PAPER GIFT SET
CLIENT DESIGN HORIZONS INTERNATIONAL

HOLIDAY

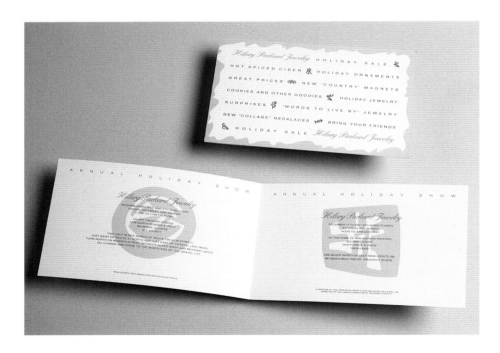

top
DESIGN FIRM STEWART MONDERER DESIGN, INC.
ART DIRECTOR STEWART MONDERER
DESIGNER ELLEN CONANT
OCCASION HOLIDAY GREETING
ILLUSTRATOR ELLEN CONANT
CLIENT STEWART MONDERER DESIGN, INC.

bottom
DESIGN FIRM MICHAEL STANARD, INC.
ART DIRECTOR LISA FINGERHUT
DESIGNER KRISTY ROBERTS
OCCASION HOLIDAY SALE
CLIENT HILARY PACKARD JEWELRY

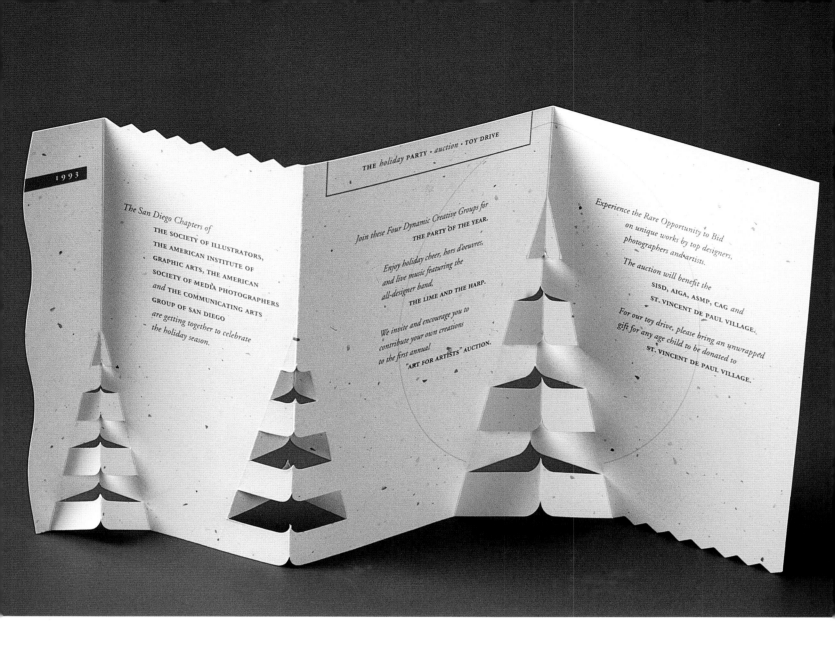

The San Diego Chapters of
THE SOCIETY OF ILLUSTRATORS,
THE AMERICAN INSTITUTE OF
GRAPHIC ARTS, THE AMERICAN
SOCIETY OF MEDIA PHOTOGRAPHERS
and THE COMMUNICATING ARTS
GROUP OF SAN DIEGO
are getting together to celebrate
the holiday season.

THE *holiday* PARTY · *auction* · TOY DRIVE

Join these Four Dynamic Creative Groups for
THE PARTY OF THE YEAR.

Enjoy holiday cheer, hors d'oeuvres,
and live music featuring the
all-designer band,
THE LIME AND THE HARP.

We invite and encourage you to
contribute your own creations
to the first annual
"ART FOR ARTISTS" AUCTION.

Experience the Rare Opportunity to Bid
on unique works by top designers,
photographers and artists.

The auction will benefit the
SISD, AIGA, ASMP, CAG and
ST. VINCENT DE PAUL VILLAGE.

For our toy drive, please bring an unwrapped
gift for any age child to be donated to
ST. VINCENT DE PAUL VILLAGE.

1993

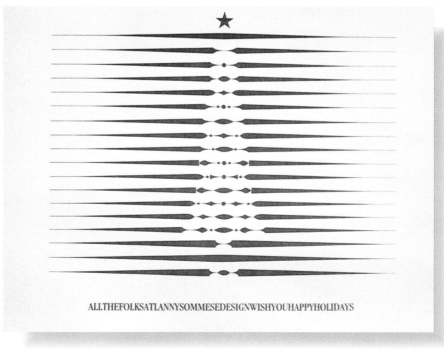

ALLTHEFOLKSATLANNYSOMMESEDESIGNWISHYOUHAPPYHOLIDAYS

top
DESIGN FIRM BENNETT PEJI DESIGN
ART DIRECTOR BENNETT PEJI
DESIGNER BENNETT PEJI
OCCASION CHRISTMAS, HOLIDAY PARTY
ILLUSTRATOR BENNETT PEJI
CLIENT AIGA/SAN DIEGO

bottom
DESIGN FIRM SOMMESE DESIGN
ART DIRECTOR LANNY SOMMESE
DESIGNER LANNY SOMMESE
OCCASION CHRISTMAS CARD
CLIENT SOMMESE DESIGN

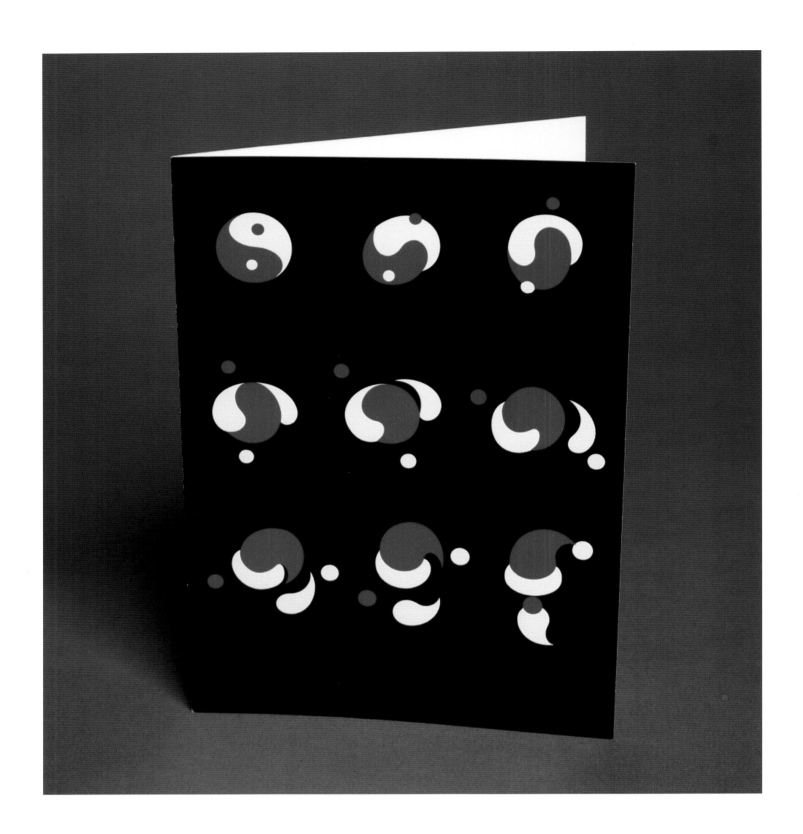

SEASON'S GREETINGS
FROM SANTA BARBARA

far left
DESIGN FIRM SUPON DESIGN GROUP, INC.
ART DIRECTOR SUPON PHORNIRUNLIT
DESIGNER RICHARD LEE HEFFNER
OCCASION CHINESE NEW YEAR
ILLUSTRATOR RICHARD LEE HEFFNER
CLIENT SUPON DESIGN GROUP, INC.

left
DESIGN FIRM SAYLES GRAPHIC DESIGN
ART DIRECTOR JOHN SAYLES
DESIGNER JOHN SAYLES
OCCASION HOLIDAY GREETING
ILLUSTRATOR JOHN SAYLES

bottom
DESIGN FIRM PUCCINELLI DESIGN
ART DIRECTOR KEITH PUCCINELLI
DESIGNER KEITH PUCCINELLI
OCCASION HOLIDAY GREETING
ILLUSTRATOR KEITH PUCCINELLI
CLIENT PUCCINELLI DESIGN

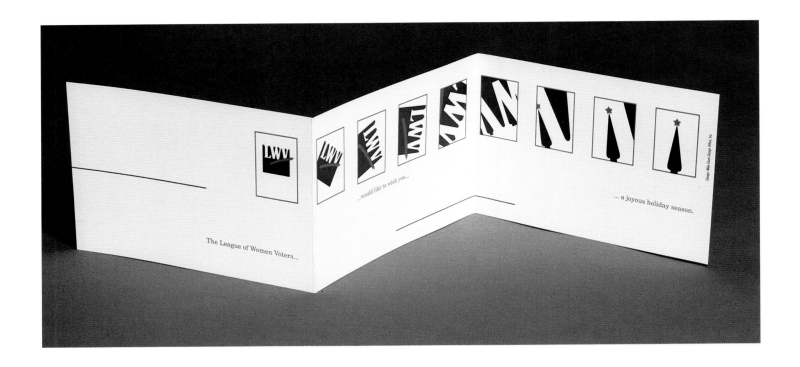

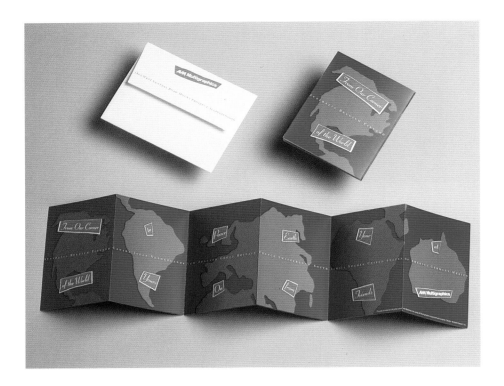

top
DESIGN FIRM MIKE QUON DESIGN OFFICE
ART DIRECTOR MIKE QUON, S. DREA
DESIGNER MIKE QUON, S. GUNN
OCCASION HOLIDAY CARDS
ILLUSTRATOR MIKE QUON, S. GUNN
CLIENT LEAGUE OF WOMEN VOTERS

bottom
DESIGN FIRM MICHAEL STANARD, INC.
ART DIRECTOR MICHAEL STANARD, INC.
DESIGNER MARC FUHRMAN
OCCASION HOLIDAY CARD
CLIENT MULTIGRAPHICS

right
DESIGN FIRM MIKE QUON DESIGN OFFICE
ART DIRECTOR MIKE QUON
DESIGNER MIKE QUON
OCCASION 'Q' LOGO, HOLIDAY CARD
PHOTOGRAPHER MIKE QUON
CLIENT MIKE QUON DESIGN OFFICE

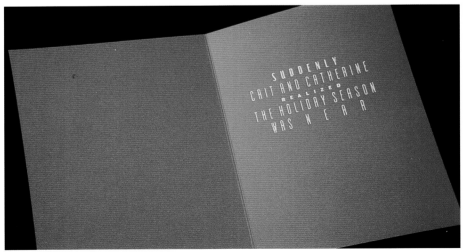

DESIGN FIRM SCHMELTZ + WARREN
ART DIRECTOR CRIT WARREN
DESIGNER CRIT WARREN
OCCASION HOLIDAY GREETING CARD
PHOTOGRAPHER CRIT WARREN
CLIENT SCHMELTZ + WARREN

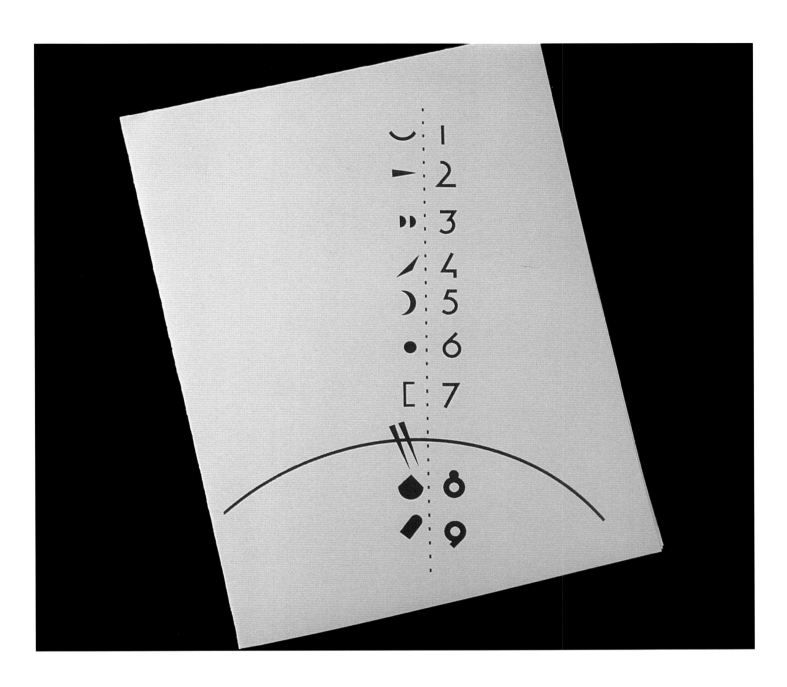

And who says art people can't add?

Happy
New Year
from
Crit+Cathy

DESIGN FIRM SCHMELTZ + WARREN
ART DIRECTOR CRIT WARREN
DESIGNER CRIT WARREN
OCCASION HOLIDAY GREETING CARD
CLIENT SCHMELTZ + WARREN

DESIGN FIRM SCHMELTZ + WARREN
ART DIRECTOR CRIT WARREN
DESIGNER CRIT WARREN
OCCASION HOLIDAY GREETING CARD
PHOTOGRAPHER CRIT WARREN
COPY: CATHERINE SCHMELTZ, CRIT WARREN
CLIENT SCHMELTZ + WARREN

feel *verb*

to view in a certain way

THIS YEAR WE WISH YOU:

Vincent receiving a letter from Theo,

AND

O. Henry's Della cutting her hair,

AND

Bing singing at the Holiday Inn.

"HARK! WE WISH YOU A HAPPY   YEAR!" SHOUTED CRIT AND CATHERINE.

DESIGN FIRM SCHMELTZ + WARREN
ART DIRECTOR CRIT WARREN
DESIGNER CRIT WARREN
OCCASION HOLIDAY GREETING CARD
CLIENT SCHMELTZ + WARREN

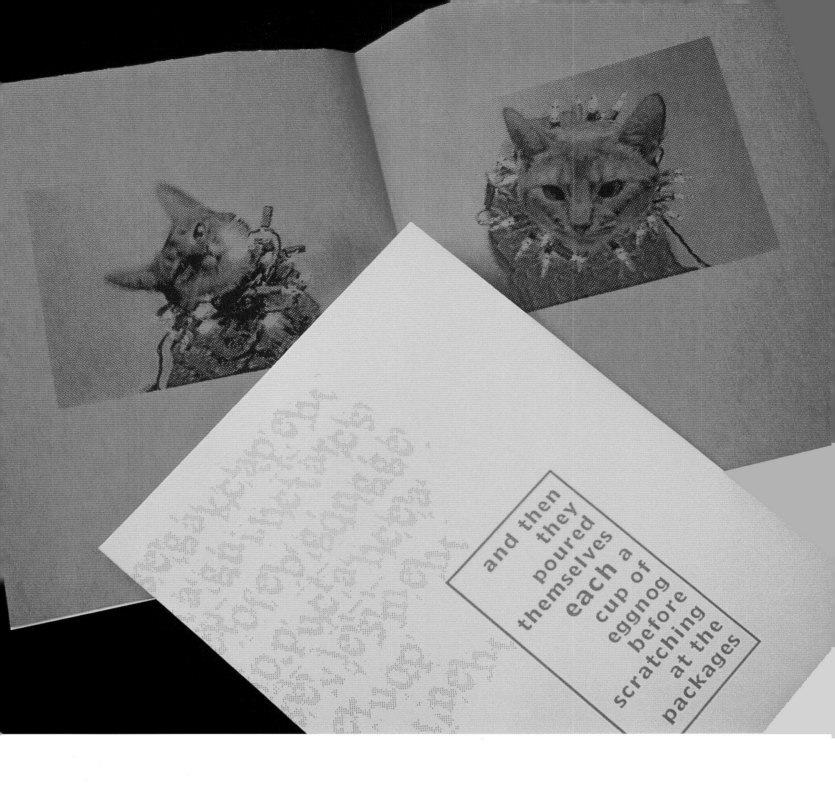

and then
they
poured
themselves
each a
cup of
eggnog
before
scratching
at the
packages

DESIGN FIRM SCHMELTZ + WARREN
ART DIRECTOR CRIT WARREN
DESIGNER CRIT WARREN
OCCASION HOLIDAY GREETING CARD
PHOTOGRAPHER CRIT WARREN
CLIENT SCHMELTZ + WARREN

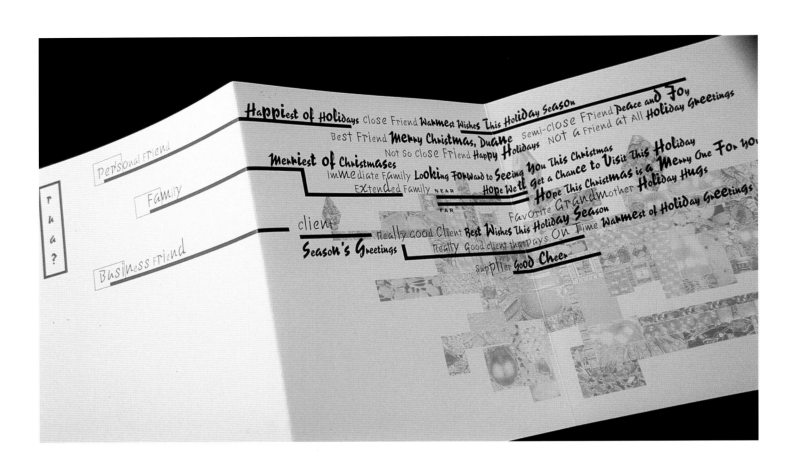

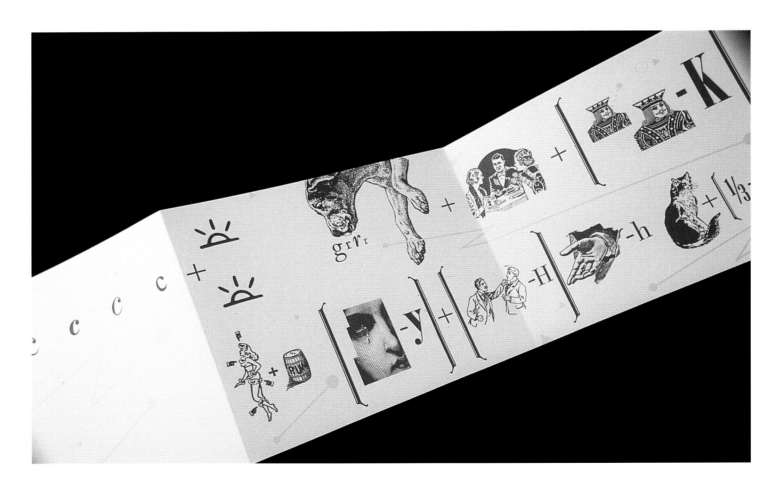

PICKLED BEETS
by Loreena McKennitt
Warner Bros. Recording Artist and Garden Lover

1/4 cup water
1/3 cup vinegar
1/4 cup sugar
1/2 teaspoon ground cinnamon
1/4 teaspoon salt
1/4 teaspoon ground cloves
2 cups sliced, cooked beets

sugar

vinegar

$

Combine water, vinegar, sugar, ground cinnamon, salt a
(Thrillseekers may also add some allspice). Heat to boiling;
cooked beets. Cover and simmer 5 minutes; chill.

VEGETARIAN MOUSSAKA
by k.d. lang
Grammy-Winning Vocalist and Vegetable Enthusiast

1 pound eggplant (thinly sliced)
pinch of salt
2 large onions, peeled and ch–
1 garlic clove (2 are –
1 cup dried

1/4 tea–

allspice or cinnamon

cream if you prefer)
pper

mesan cheese

d dry.
. Add the garlic,

pepper.

on each side

er with half

neg. Pour

WARNER BROS. RECORDS
proudly presents

Holiday
Favorites

Recipes from the Family of Warner Bros. Records Recording Artists

left top
DESIGN FIRM SCHMELTZ + WARREN
ART DIRECTOR CRIT WARREN
DESIGNER CRIT WARREN
OCCASION HOLIDAY GREETING CARD
CLIENT SCHMELTZ + WARREN

left bottom
DESIGN FIRM SCHMELTZ + WARREN
ART DIRECTOR CRIT WARREN
DESIGNER CRIT WARREN
OCCASION HOLIDAY GREETING CARD
PHOTOGRAPHER CRIT WARREN
CLIENT SCHMELTZ + WARREN

above
DESIGN FIRM MODERN DOG
ART DIRECTOR JERI HEIDEN
DESIGNER ROBYNNE RAYE, MICHAEL STRASSBURGER
OCCASION HOLIDAY CARD
ILLUSTRATOR ROBYNNE RAYE
CLIENT WARNER BROTHERS RECORDS

top
DESIGN FIRM SIBLEY/PETEET DESIGN, INC.
ART DIRECTOR REX PETEET
DESIGNER REX PETEET
OCCASION CHRISTMAS CARD
ILLUSTRATOR REX PETEET
CLIENT SIBLEY/PETEET DESIGN, INC.

top
DESIGN FIRM MARK OLDACH DESIGN
ART DIRECTOR MARK OLDACH
DESIGNER MARK MEYER
OCCASION CHRISTMAS CARD
CLIENT FIRST IMPRESSION

left
DESIGN FIRM SOMMESE DESIGN
ART DIRECTOR KRISTIN SOMMESE,
  LANNY SOMMESE
DESIGNER KRISTIN SOMMESE
OCCASION SEASON'S GREETINGS POSTCARD
ILLUSTRATOR LANNY SOMMESE
CLIENT SOMMESE DESIGN

酉

SUPON
DESIGN
GROUP
WISHES
YOU
GOOD
FORTUNE
AND
HEALTH
THROUGHOUT
1993

left
DESIGN FIRM SAYLES GRAPHIC DESIGN
ART DIRECTOR JOHN SAYLES
DESIGNER JOHN SAYLES
OCCASION HOLIDAY GREETING
ILLUSTRATOR JOHN SAYLES
CLIENT SAYLES GRAPHIC DESIGN

below
DESIGN FIRM BULLET COMMUNICATIONS, INC.
ART DIRECTOR TIM SCOTT
DESIGNER TIM SCOTT
OCCASION HOLIDAY DESSERT PARTY
CLIENT THE JOHN BUCK MANAGEMENT GROUP

right
DESIGN FIRM SUPON DESIGN GROUP, INC.
ART DIRECTOR SUPON PHORNIRUNLIT
DESIGNER RICHARD LEE HEFFNER
OCCASION CHINESE NEW YEAR
ILLUSTRATOR RICHARD LEE HEFFNER
CLIENT SUPON DESIGN GROUP, INC.

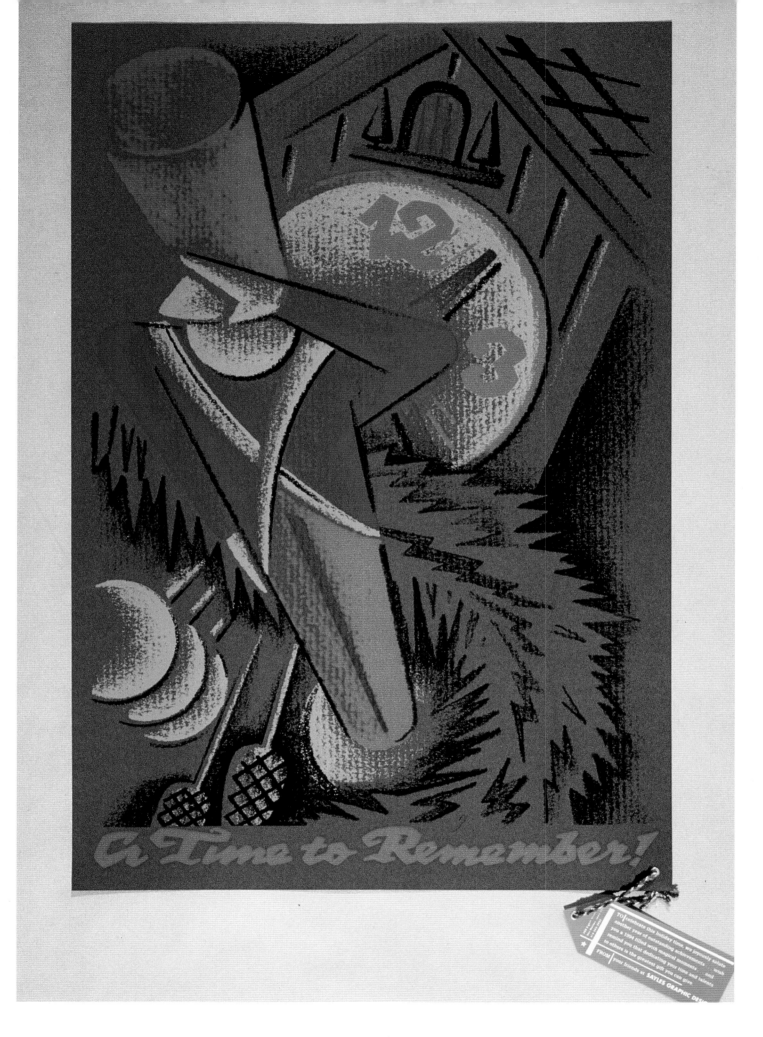

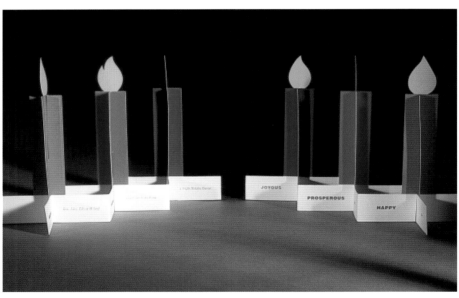

above
DESIGN FIRM CHERMAYEFF & GEISMAR, INC.
ART DIRECTOR STEFF GEISSBUHLER
DESIGNER STEFF GEISSBUHLER, LISETTE BUIANI
OCCASION HOLIDAY CARD
CLIENT ANCHOR ENGRAVING & FAMILY OF STEFF
GEISSBUHLER

right top
DESIGN FIRM MODERN DOG
ART DIRECTOR MICHAEL STRASSBURGER,
ROBYNNE RAYE
DESIGNER MICHAEL STRASSBURGER
OCCASION HOLIDAY (CHRISTMAS)
ILLUSTRATOR MICHAEL STRASSBURGER
CLIENT MODERN DOG

right bottom
DESIGN FIRM STEWART MONDERER DESIGN, INC.
ART DIRECTOR STEWART MONDERER
DESIGNER ROBERT DAVISON
OCCASION HOLIDAY/NEW YEAR'S CARD
CLIENT STEWART MONDERER DESIGN, INC.

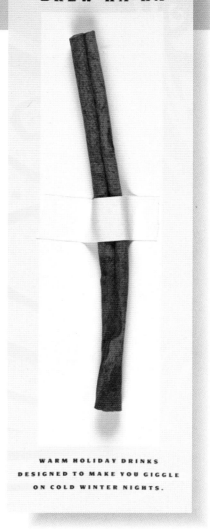

left
DESIGN FIRM DBD INTERNATIONAL LTD.
ART DIRECTOR DAVID BRIER
DESIGNER DAVID BRIER
OCCASION CHRISTMAS
ILLUSTRATOR DAVID BRIER
CLIENT DBD INTERNATIONAL LTD.

right
DESIGN FIRM JAVIER ROMERO DESIGN GROUP
ART DIRECTOR JAVIER ROMERO
OCCASION SEASONAL PROMOTION
PHOTOGRAPHER JOSEPH SACHS
CLIENT SELF PROMOTIONAL

top
DESIGN FIRM SUPON DESIGN GROUP, INC.
ART DIRECTOR SUPON PHORNIRUNLIT
DESIGNER ANDREW DOLAN, DIANNE COOK,
 JOHN COLEMAN, NELTON CASTRO
OCCASION SEASON'S GREETINGS
CLIENT SUPON DESIGN GROUP

bottom
DESIGN FIRM THE DUNLAVEY STUDIO, INC.
ART DIRECTOR MICHAEL DUNLAVEY
DESIGNER LINDY DUNLAVEY
OCCASION CHRISTMAS CARD
PHOTOGRAPHER IZZY SWARTZ (PHOTO OF PIECE)
ILLUSTRATOR CHAPBOOK
CLIENT THE DUNLAVEY STUDIO, INC.
THE INSIDE WAS XEROXED OUT OF A BIBLE, THEN
CRUMBLED. THE RIBBON WAS HAND
STITCHED BY ONE OF THE STAFF AND THE WHILE
BOOK WAS PRINTED ON A LETTERPRESS.

right
DESIGN FIRM SUPON DESIGN GROUP, INC.
ART DIRECTOR SUPON PHORNIRUNLIT
DESIGNER ANDREW DOLAN, DIANNE COOK,
 DAVE PRESCOTT
OCCASION NEW YEARS GIFT
CLIENT SUPON DESIGN GROUP, INC.

The snowballs package text reads (partially legible):

CORMAC DUNLAVEY, OUR INTREPID FOUNDER, LEFT IRELAND IN 1848 AND DECIDED TO MAKE HIS FORTUNE IN ALASKA, BUT ALL HE ENDED UP MAKING WAS SNOWBALLS. AND SINCE THOSE MELTED EVERY SPRING, THEY WEREN'T EXACTLY SOMETHING YOU COULD TAKE TO THE BANK. AT LEAST NOT UNTIL HE DISCOVERED HOW TO MAKE THEM LAST VIRTUALLY FOREVER. THEN CAME THE SUCCESS HE HAD DREAMED OF. NOW OUR STUDIO, HIS LEGACY, IS PROUD TO PRESENT THE PRODUCT THAT MADE CORMAC'S NAME WHAT IT IS TODAY. AND IF YOU ARE AS INTREPID AS CORMAC, YOU MIGHT EVEN EAT THESE SNOWBALLS. IF YOU'RE NOT, TRY GLUING THEM TOGETHER AND MAKING THEM INTO A TREE ORNAMENT THAT GLOWS IN THE DARK, OR THROW IT AT SOME UNSUSPECTING PASSER-BY, WHO WON'T STAND A SNOWBALL'S CHANCE OF DUCKING CORMAC'S BEST.

We Wish You a Yummy Christmas

THE DUNLAVEY STUDIO

SnowBalls
CHRISTMAS 1995
The Dunlavey Studio

INSIDE THIS BOX, YOU WILL DISCOVER THE THRILLING STORY OF THE DUNLAVEY STUDIO'S ADVENTUROUS FOUNDER, CORMAC DUNLAVEY. AND IN CELEBRATION OF THE SEASON, WE ARE HONORED TO PRESENT A TREAT THAT ONLY THE LEGENDARY CORMAC COULD HAVE CONCEIVED OF. WITH HIS INSPIRATION, WE WISH YOU A HOLIDAY OF JOY AND WONDER.

The Dunlavey Studio
PLEASE DELIVER TO:

POOCH Pâté

top
DESIGN FIRM THE DUNLAVEY STUDIO, INC.
ART DIRECTOR MICHAEL DUNLAVEY
DESIGNER LINDY DUNLAVEY
OCCASION CHRISTMAS SNOWBALLS PACKAGE
CLIENT THE DUNLAVEY STUDIO, INC.

bottom
DESIGN FIRM PUCCINELLI DESIGN
ART DIRECTOR KEITH PUCCINELLI
DESIGNER KEITH PUCCINELLI
OCCASION HOLIDAY SELF PROMOTION
ILLUSTRATOR KEITH PUCCINELLI
CLIENT PUCCINELLI DESIGN

DESIGN FIRM ABRAMS DESIGN GROUP
ART DIRECTOR COLLEEN ABRAMS
DESIGNER DAVID ROSE, PAULA PEREZ,
  ANDREA LEWAK, ELAINE GOLDSTONE,
  KAY WATANABE
OCCASION HOLIDAY PROMOTION
PHOTOGRAPHER JEFF HURN
ILLUSTRATOR DAVID ROSE, PAULA PEREZ,
  ANDREA LEWAK, ELAINE GOLDSTONE,
  KAY WATANABE
CLIENT ABRAMS DESIGN GROUP

HOLIDAY

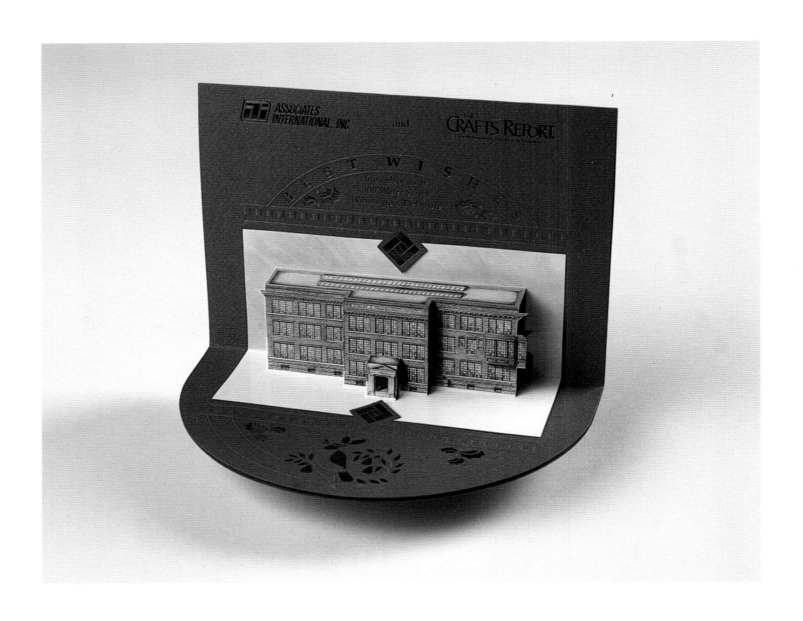

left
DESIGN FIRM JUSTINTIME DIMENSIONAL
  GREETING CARDS
ART DIRECTOR WILLIAM R. IVES
DESIGNER WILLIAM R. IVES
OCCASION CHRISTMAS CARD
ILLUSTRATOR RICHARD MARCHAND
CLIENT ASSOCIATE'S INTERNATIONAL

right
DESIGN FIRM SUPON DESIGN GROUP, INC.
ART DIRECTOR SUPON PHORNIRUNLIT,
  ANDREW DOLAN
DESIGNER RICHARD BOYNTON
OCCASION GREETING CARD PACKAGE
ILLUSTRATOR PATRICK O'BRIEN
CLIENT SUPON DESIGN GROUP, INC.
THIS POCKET FOLDER, WITH FOUR POCKETS,
CONTAINS STATIONERY FOR EACH SEASON.

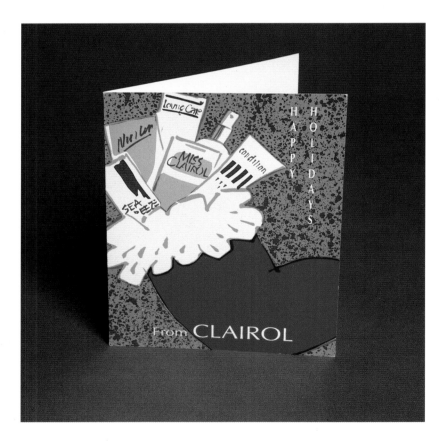

top
DESIGN FIRM SOMMESE DESIGN
ART DIRECTOR KRISTIN SOMMESE
DESIGNER KRISTIN SOMMESE
OCCASION GREETING CARDS
CLIENT CUT CARDS, INC.
DIE CUT CARDS FEATURE "PENNSYLVANIA STATE
UNIVERSITY LANDMARKS.

bottom
DESIGN FIRM MIKE QUON DESIGN OFFICE
DESIGNER MIKE QUON
OCCASION PROMOTION
ILLUSTRATOR MIKE QUON
CLIENT TARTARO SLAVIN INC.

HOLIDAY MEMORIES FROM PRINT NORTHWEST

OH, THE WONDER AND MAGIC OF THE SEASON. GRANDDAD'S TRAIN, A GIFT FROM A HOLIDAY PAST, WHISTLES ... TREE. GARLANDS OF ... AND RED SATIN BALLS INTO ITS BOUGHS.

AN HEIRLOOM ANGEL WATCHES OVER FROM ABOVE. CAROLERS IN PLUSH VELVET DRESSES AND TOP HATS COME A WASSAILING. SNOW COVERS THE FIRST FALLEN ... GLISTENING THE LAND WITH A WHITE ROBE. SO MUCH YOU CAN'T. REINDEERS PRANCING ON ROOFTOPS. TOY SOLDIERS PARADING IN THE NIGHT. THE PEACE AND GOODWILL THAT FILL UP YOUR HEART WITH JOY.

DESIGN FIRM HORNALL ANDERSON DESIGN WORKS
ART DIRECTOR JACK ANDERSON
DESIGNER JACK ANDERSON, HEIDI HATLESTAD, JULIA LAPINE, LIAN NG
OCCASION HOLIDAY GREETING CARD
CLIENT PRINT NORTHWEST

top .
DESIGN FIRM RICKABAUGH GRAPHICS
ART DIRECTOR ERIC RICKABAUGH
DESIGNER MICHAEL TENNYSON SMITH
OCCASION HOLIDAY CARD
ILLUSTRATOR MICHAEL TENNYSON SMITH
CLIENT RICKABAUGH GRAPHICS
THE COVER TITLE WAS HAND TIPPED, WOOD
BINDING WAS HAND SEWN, AND THE EDGE WAS
HAND TORN.

right
DESIGN FIRM DESIGN HORIZONS
 INTERNATIONAL
ART DIRECTOR BRYAN SANZOTTI
DESIGNER KRISTA FERDINAND
OCCASION HOLIDAY PROMOTION/GREETING
 CARD
ILLUSTRATOR KRISTA FERDINAND
CLIENT DESIGN HORIZONS INTERNATIONAL

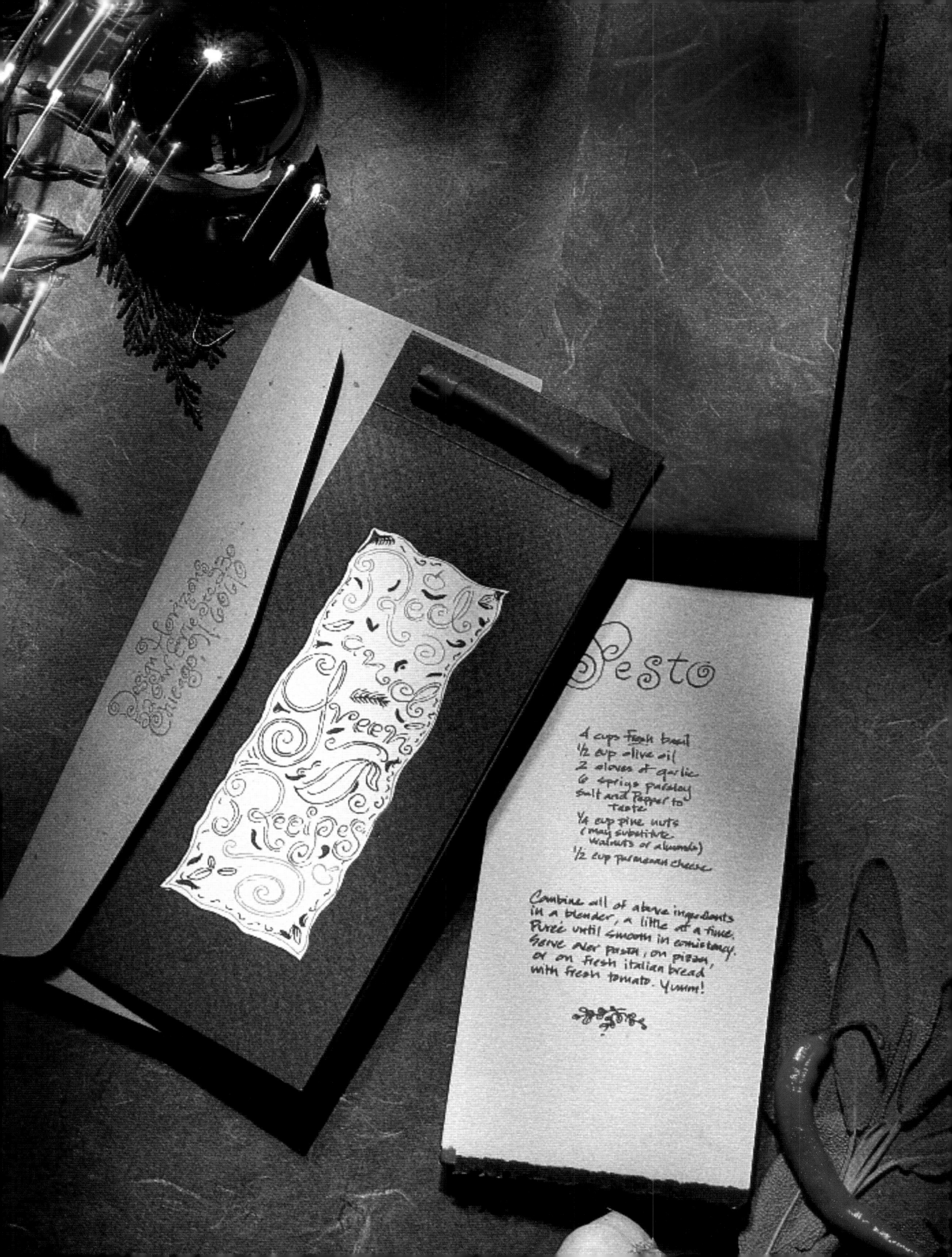

Peel and Green Recipes

Pesto

4 cups fresh basil
1/2 cup olive oil
2 cloves of garlic
6 sprigs parsley
Salt and Pepper to
    taste
1/4 cup pine nuts
   (may substitute
    walnuts or almonds)
1/2 cup parmesan cheese

Combine all of above ingredients
in a blender, a little at a time.
Purée until smooth in consistency.
Serve over pasta, on pizza,
or on fresh Italian bread
with fresh tomato. Yumm!

CONFIDENT at forty-six.

Surrounded by success.

And family.

Of self-determined quality.

Yet humble to acknowledge

was not done alone.

Thanking.

Not asking.

Not resolving.

Letting the moment go.

for others to capture.

Looking back.

Relaxed.

AFTER MIDNIGHT.

MIDNIGHT
December 31. Evermore

Holiday Gala

top
DESIGN FIRM MARK OLDACH DESIGN
ART DIRECTOR MARK OLDACH
DESIGNER MARK OLDACH
OCCASION NEW YEAR'S CARD
PHOTOGRAPHER ANTHONY ARCIERO
CLIENT MARK OLDACH DESIGN

bottom
DESIGN FIRM JULIA TAM DESIGN
ART DIRECTOR JULIA CHONG TAM
DESIGNER JULIA CHONG TAM
OCCASION CHRISTMAS PARTY INVITATION
ILLUSTRATOR JULIA CHONG TAM
CLIENT UCLA GRADUATE SCHOOL OF
    EDUCATION

HOLIDAY

The first champagne glass was modeled after Marie Antoinette's cleavage.

SAVOR THE HOLIDAYS

from the employees of
CENTRE REINSURANCE
and
ZURICH INTERNATIONAL (BERMUDA) LTD.

DESIGN FIRM WYD DESIGN, INC.
ART DIRECTOR FRANK J. OSWALD
DESIGNER DAVID DUNKELBERGER, JANET EUSEBIO
OCCASION CENTRE RE HOLIDAY GREETING
CLIENT CENTRE REINSURANCE COMPANIES

above
Design Firm Mires Design, Inc.
Art Director José Serrano
Occasion Christmas Card
Client Mires Design, Inc.

DESIGN FIRM PAUL DAVIS STUDIO
ART DIRECTOR PAUL DAVIS
DESIGNER PAUL DAVIS
ILLUSTRATOR PAUL DAVIS
CLIENT PAUL DAVIS

HOLIDAY

left
DESIGN FIRM RICKABAUGH GRAPHICS
ART DIRECTOR ERIC RICKABAUGH
DESIGNER ERIC RICKABAUGH
OCCASION HOLIDAY CARD/MOVING
    ANNOUNCEMENT
CLIENT RICKABAUGH GRAPHICS

right
DESIGN FIRM SAYLES GRAPHIC DESIGN
ART DIRECTOR JOHN SAYLES DESIGN
DESIGNER JOHN SAYLES
OCCASION HOLIDAY GREETING
ILLUSTRATOR JOHN SAYLES
CLIENT SAYLES GRAPHIC DESIGN

'TIS A MAGICAL VISION, A WONDROUS SIGHT, OUR FAMILY TREE WITH ITS GLORIOUS LIGHT!

OUR FAMILY TREE

SO STRONG, ITS BRANCHES, SO BRIGHT, ITS STAR, BRINGING CHEER AND BEST WISHES TO FRIENDS, FROM AFAR.

SAYLES GRAPHIC DESIGN, INC.

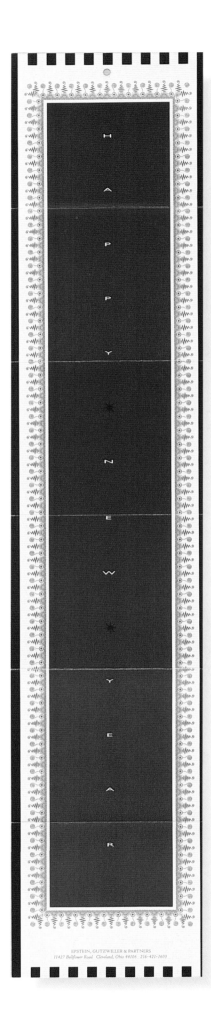

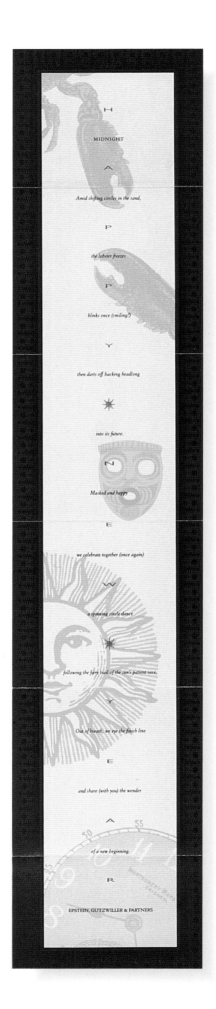

left
DESIGN FIRM EPSTEIN, GUTZWILLER, SCHULTZ AND PARTNERS
ART DIRECTOR ANNE KELEMEN, SYLVIE HANNA
DESIGNER ANNE KELEMEN, SYLVIE HANNA
OCCASION NEW YEARS CARD
CLIENT EPSTEIN, GUTZWILLER, SCHULTZ AND PARTNERS

top right
DESIGN FIRM APRIL GREIMAN ASSOCIATES
ART DIRECTOR APRIL GREIMAN
DESIGNER APRIL GREIMAN
OCCASION YEARLY GREETING
PHOTOGRAPHER APRIL GREIMAN
ILLUSTRATOR APRIL GREIMAN
CLIENT APRIL GREIMAN ASSOCIATES

bottom right
DESIGN FIRM THE DUNLAVEY STUDIO, INC.
ART DIRECTOR MICHAEL DUNLAVEY
DESIGNER LINDY DUNLAVEY
OCCASION CHRISTMAS CARD
CLIENT THE DUNLAVEY STUDIO, INC.

Creativity, common sense and love do come together in one fundamental sense. The three of them happen when you reach the point of awareness where you let go of something and let something else emerge.

Francisco Varela

top
DESIGN FIRM SOMMESE DESIGN
ART DIRECTOR KRISTIN SOMMESE, LANNY SOMMESE
DESIGNER KRISTIN SOMMESE
OCCASION ANNUAL HALLOWEEN COSTUME PARTY
 INVITATION
ILLUSTRATOR LANNY SOMMESE
CLIENT SOMMESE DESIGN

bottom
DESIGN FIRM SOMMESE DESIGN
ART DIRECTOR KRISTIN SOMMESE, LANNY SOMMESE
DESIGNER KRISTIN SOMMESE
OCCASION ANNUAL HALLOWEEN COSTUME PARTY
ILLUSTRATOR LANNY SOMMESE
CLIENT SOMMESE DESIGN

LANNY & KRISTIN INVITE YOU TO THEIR ANNUAL
HALLOWEEN COSTUME BASH — OCTOBER 27, 9PM

DESIGN FIRM SOMMESE DESIGN
ART DIRECTOR KRISTIN SOMMESE, LANNY SOMMESE
DESIGNER KRISTIN SOMMESE
OCCASION ANNUAL HALLOWEEN COSTUME PARTY
ILLUSTRATOR LANNY SOMMESE
CLIENT SOMMESE DESIGN

DESIGN FIRM SMULLEN DESIGN
DESIGNER MAUREEN SMULLEN
OCCASION HALLOWEEN SELF PROMOTION
CLIENT SMULLEN DESIGN

Wishing You

Happy Tricks

Delicious Treats

And Big Fun on the 31st.

ColemanSouter

DESIGN FIRM COLEMAN SOUTER
ART DIRECTOR MARK COLEMAN
DESIGNER ERIK WATTS
OCCASION HALLOWEEN
ILLUSTRATOR ERIK WATTS
CLIENT COLEMAN SOUTER

left
DESIGN FIRM HORNALL ANDERSON DESIGN WORKS
ART DIRECTOR JACK ANDERSON
DESIGNER JACK ANDERSON, JULIE TANAGI-LOCK,
  LIAN NG
OCCASION WASHINGTON SOFTWARE
  ASSOCIATION HALLOWEEN BALL
ILLUSTRATOR JULIA LAPINE
CLIENT WASHINGTON SOFTWARE ASSOCIATION

right
DESIGN FIRM SOMMESE DESIGN
ART DIRECTOR KRISTIN SOMMESE, LANNY SOMMESE
DESIGNER KRISTIN SOMMESE
OCCASION ANNUAL HALLOWEEN COSTUME PARTY
ILLUSTRATOR LANNY SOMMESE
CLIENT SOMMESE DESIGN & FRIENDS

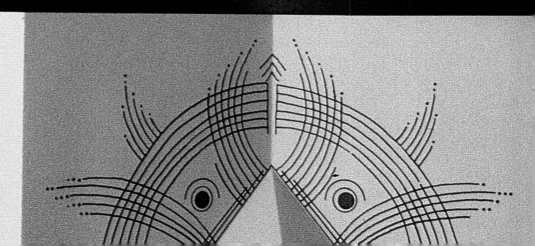

MISCELLANEOUS

GOOD NATURE DESIGNS™

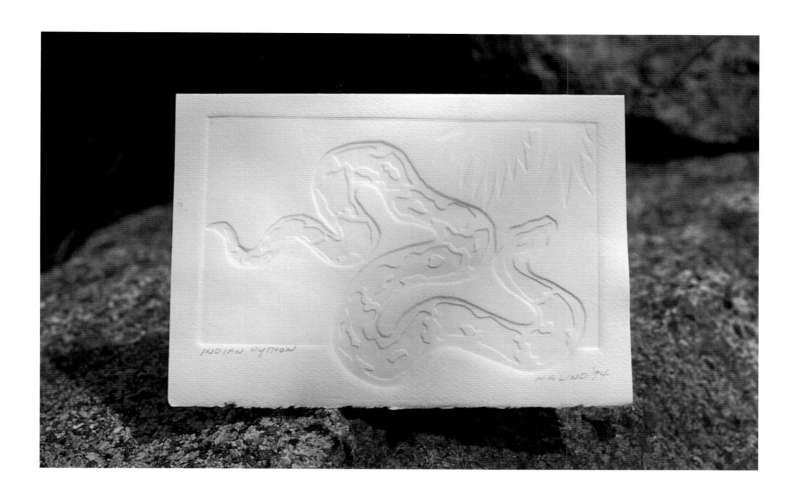

far left
DESIGN FIRM SIEBERT DESIGN ASSOCIATES
ART DIRECTOR LORI SIEBERT
DESIGNER BARB RAYMOND, LORI SIEBERT,
 DAVID CARROLL, LISA BALLARD
OCCASION ALL OCCASION NOTES
ILLUSTRATOR BARB RAYMOND, LORI SIEBERT,
 DAVID CARROLL, LISA BALLARD
CLIENT GOOD NATURE DESIGNS

top
DESIGN FIRM LIND ADVERTISING
ART DIRECTOR H.A. LIND
DESIGNER H.A. LIND
ILLUSTRATOR H.A. LIND
CLIENT LIND ADVERTISING
SNAKE IMAGE COLLAGRAPH PRODUCED
ON AN ETCHING PRESS.

bottom
DESIGN FIRM LIND ADVERTISING
ART DIRECTOR H.A. LIND
DESIGNER H.A. LIND
ILLUSTRATOR H.A. LIND
CLIENT LIND ADVERTISING

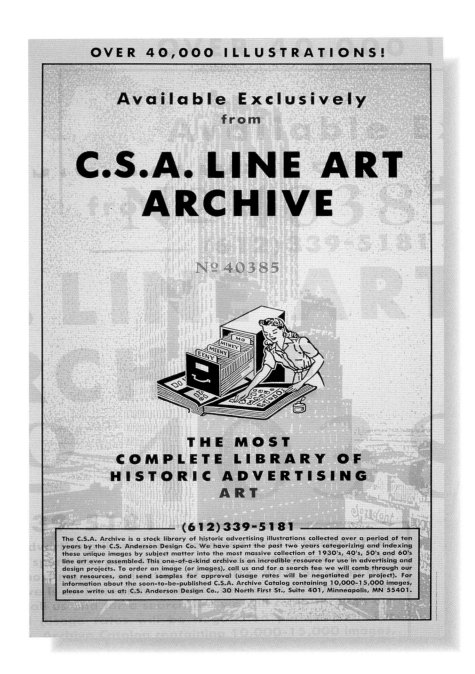

OVER 40,000 ILLUSTRATIONS!

Available Exclusively
from

C.S.A. LINE ART ARCHIVE

№ 40385

THE MOST COMPLETE LIBRARY OF HISTORIC ADVERTISING ART

(612)339-5181

The C.S.A. Archive is a stock library of historic advertising illustrations collected over a period of ten years by the C.S. Anderson Design Co. We have spent the past two years categorizing and indexing these unique images by subject matter into the most massive collection of 1930's, 40's, 50's and 60's line art ever assembled. This one-of-a-kind archive is an incredible resource for use in advertising and design projects. To order an image (or images), call us and for a search fee we will comb through our vast resources, and send samples for approval (usage rates will be negotiated per project). For information about the soon-to-be-published C.S.A. Archive Catalog containing 10,000-15,000 images, please write us at: C.S. Anderson Design Co., 30 North First St., Suite 401, Minneapolis, MN 55401.

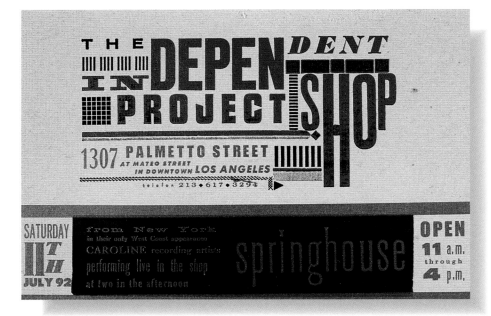

GLOBAL

EMBRACING ALL
CONSIDERATIONS,
CASES OR VALUES

G

CUSTOM

MPLS
MINN
55401

C

28/11

MADE TO IND-
IVIDUAL REQUIRE-
MENTS OR NEEDS

CSA DESIGN

TO INTRODUC
A NEW IDEA, METHOD, OR
DEVICE; TO EFFECT CHANGE

MPLS
MINN

I

INNOVATIVE

TV

CSA DESIGN

JULO
GT

300
500

N.C.

THOROUGH AT-
TENTION TO ALL ELE-
MENTS OF THE WHOLE

DETAILED

ESTAB.
MINNEAPOLIS
MINNESOTA

D

above
DESIGN FIRM CHARLES S. ANDERSON DESIGN CO.
ART DIRECTOR CHARLES S. ANDERSON
DESIGNER CHARLES S. ANDERSON, DANIEL OLSON,
 TODD HAUSWIRTH
OCCASION PROMOTIONAL ANNOUNCEMENT
COPY LISA PEMRICK
ILLUSTRATOR RANDALL DAHLK
CLIENT CHARLES S. ANDERSON DESIGN CO.

Design Firm Rickabaugh Graphics
Art Director Eric Rickabaugh
Designer Tina Zientarski
Occasion Chocolate Fantasy Fair Invitation
Client Huntington Trust Company

DESIGN FIRM RICKABAUGH GRAPHICS
ART DIRECTOR ERIC RICKABAUGH
DESIGNER MARK KRUMEL
OCCASION ANNUAL MEETING
CLIENT OHIO ARTS COUNCIL

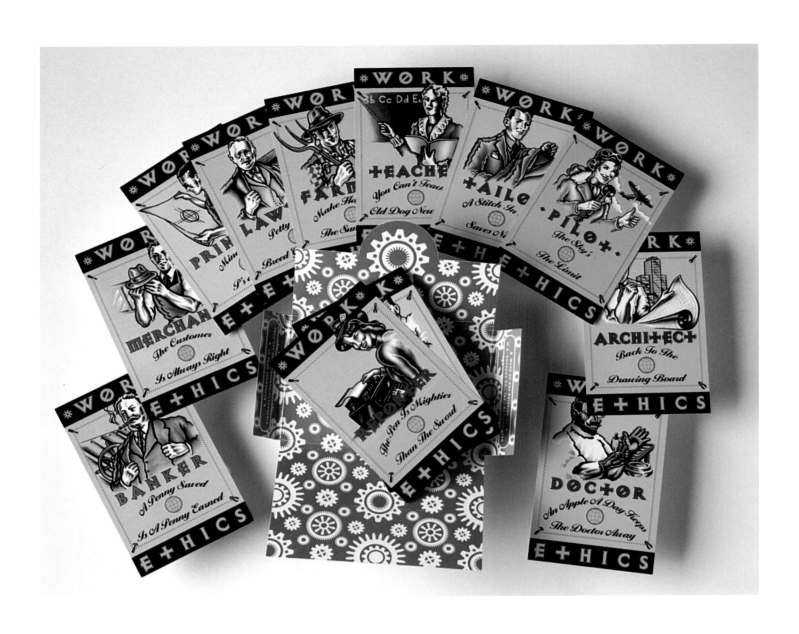

DESIGN FIRM MIDNIGHT OIL STUDIOS
ART DIRECTOR JAMES SKILES
DESIGNER JAMES SKILES
OCCASION SELF-PROMOTION
ILLUSTRATOR TIM MCGRATH
CLIENT MIDNIGHT OIL STUDIOS

top
DESIGN FIRM THE DUNLAVEY STUDIO, INC.
ART DIRECTOR MICHAEL DUNLAVEY
DESIGNER LINDY DUNLAVEY
OCCASION ST. PATRICK'S DAY
  SELF-PROMOTIONAL IRISH PAPERWEIGHT
CLIENT THE DUNLAVEY STUDIO, INC.

bottom
DESIGN FIRM SAYLES GRAPHIC DESIGN
ART DIRECTOR JOHN SAYLES
DESIGNER JOHN SAYLES
OCCASION "WE'RE SAVING A PLACE FOR YOU"
ILLUSTRATOR JOHN SAYLES
CLIENT PALMER COMMUNICATIONS

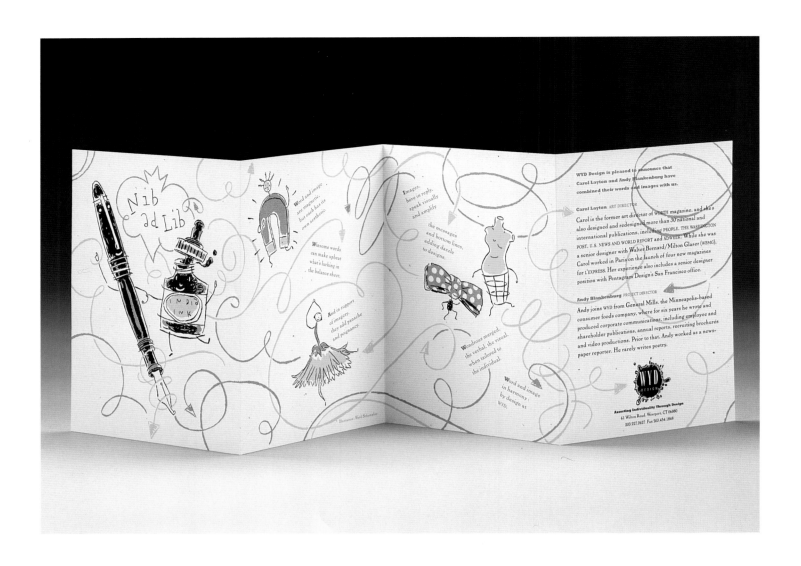

top
Design Firm WYD Design, Inc.
Art Director Frank J. Oswald
Designer Carol Layton
Occasion "Nib Ad Lib" Promotion
Illustrator Ward Schumaker
Client WYD Design, Inc.
Copywriter Andy Blankenburg

bottom
Design Firm Mike Quon Design Office
Designer Mike Quon
Occasion Promotion
Illustrator Mike Quon
Client Tartaro Slavin Inc.

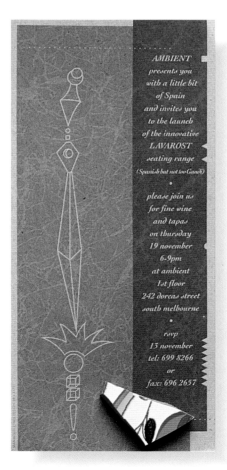

top
DESIGN FIRM MIKE QUON DESIGN OFFICE
ART DIRECTOR FRANK BERNARDUCCI
DESIGNER MIKE QUON
OCCASION ART AGAINST DRUGS PROMOTION
ILLUSTRATOR MIKE QUON
CLIENT FRANK BERNARDUCCI GALLERY

bottom
DESIGN FIRM MAMMOLITI CHAN DESIGN
ART DIRECTOR TONY MAMMOLITI
DESIGNER TONY MAMMOLITI
OCCASION AMBIENT LAVAROST (SPANISH)
   SEATING LAUNCH
ILLUSTRATOR TONY MAMMOLITI
CLIENT AMBIENT CONTRACT INTERIORS PTY. LTD.
A TILE CHIP WAS GLUED TO THE INVITATION

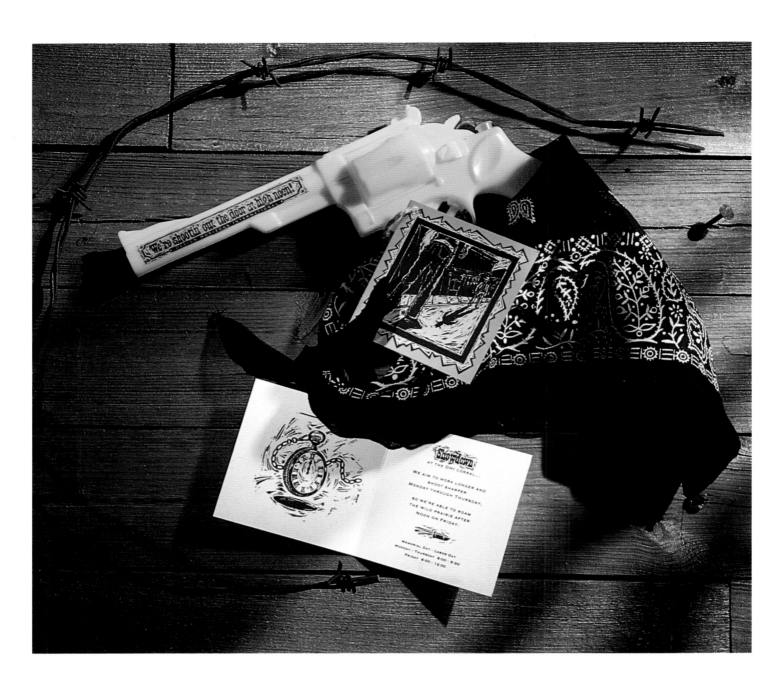

top
DESIGN FIRM DESIGN HORIZONS INTERNATIONAL
ART DIRECTOR BRYANN SANZOTTI
DESIGNER JANAN CAIN
OCCASION SUMMER PROMOTION
ILLUSTRATOR JANAN CAIN
CLIENT DESIGN HORIZONS INTERNATIONAL

bottom
DESIGN FIRM HEATHER ROBINET
DESIGNER HEATHER ROBINET
OCCASION GRAPHIC DESIGNER'S PROMOTION

right
DESIGN FIRM CHARLES S. ANDERSON DESIGN CO.
ART DIRECTOR CHARLES S. ANDERSON
DESIGNER CHARLES S. ANDERSON, JENNIFER BAER
OCCASION ANNOUNCE NEW WATCHES
ILLUSTRATOR CSA ARCHIVE
CLIENT CHARLES S. ANDERSON DESIGN CO.

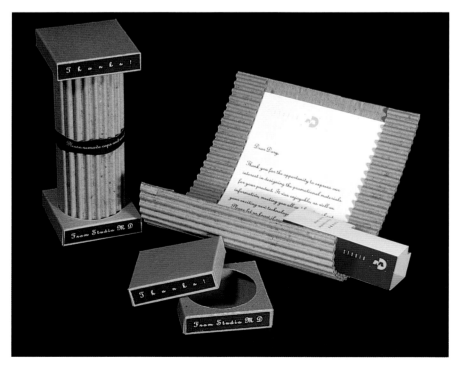

top
DESIGN FIRM MIRES DESIGN, INC.
ART DIRECTOR SCOTT MIRES
DESIGNER SCOTT MIRES
OCCASION PROMOTIONAL
CLIENT HARCOURT BRACE & JOVANOVICH

bottom
DESIGN FIRM STUDIO MD
ART DIRECTOR JESSE DOQUILO, RANDY LIM,
GLENN MITSUI
DESIGNER JESSE DOQUILO
OCCASION THANK YOU CARDS
CLIENT STUDIO MD

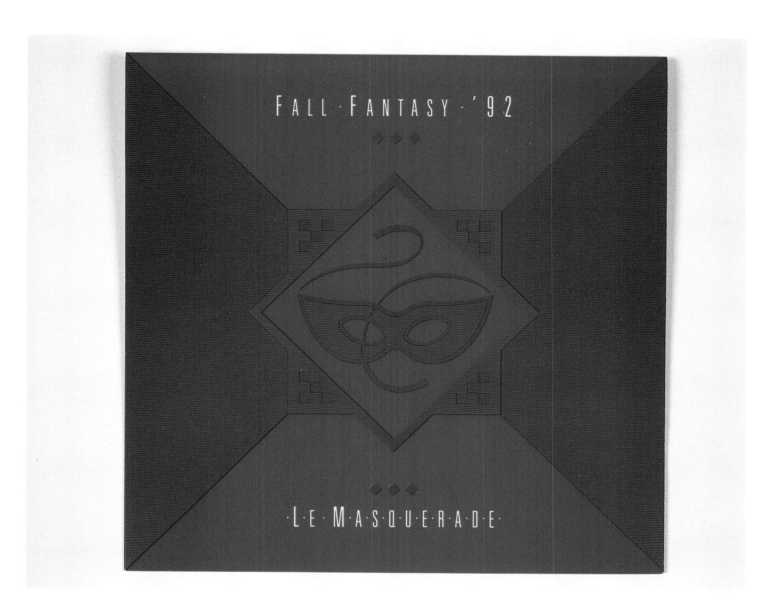

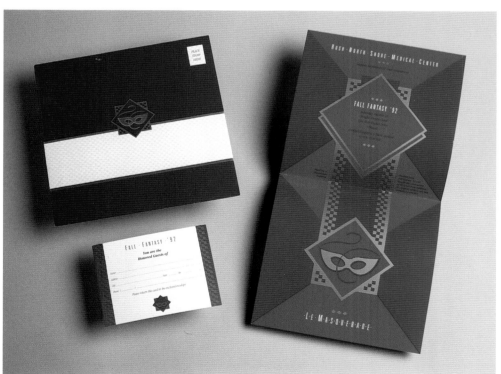

DESIGN FIRM WATTS DESIGN, INC.
ART DIRECTOR ED WATTS
DESIGNER ED WATTS
OCCASION HOSPITAL BENEFIT
CLIENT RUSH NORTH SHORE MEDICAL CENTER

DESIGN DIRECTORY

Abrams Design Group
100 View Street, Ste. 203
Mountainview, CA 94041

Charles S. Anderson Design Co.
30 North 1st Street, #400
Minneapolis, MN 55401

Beckman Corporate Graphics Center
2500 Harbor Blvd.
Fullerton, CA 92634

Bennett Peji Design
5145 Rebel Road
San Diego, CA 92117

Boelts Bros. Design Inc.
14 East 2nd Street
Tucson, AZ 85705

John Brady Design Consultants
3 Gateway Center, 17th Floor
Pittsburgh, PA 15222

Bullet Communications, Inc.
666 West Oakdale Avenue
Chicago, IL 60657

Chermayeff & Geismar, Inc.
15 East 26th Street
New York, NY 10010

Coleman Souter
591 Howard Street
San Francisco, CA 94133

DBD International Ltd.
38 Park Avenue
Rutherford, NJ 07070

Paul Davis Studio
14 East 4th Street, #504
New York, NY 10012

Design Horizons International
520 West Erie, Suite 230
Chicago, IL 60610

The Dunlavey Studio
3576 McKinley Blvd.
Sacramento, CA 95816

The Dynamic Duo, Inc.
95 Kings Highway South
Westport, CT 06880

Eikon Creations
919 Metro Centre II
21 Lam Hing Street
Kowloon, Hong Kong

Epstein, Gutziller, Schultz and Partners
11427 Bellflower Road
Cleveland, OH 44106

Farenheit
169 West Newton
Boston, MA 02118-1204

April Greiman Associates
620 Moulton Avenue, #211
Los Angeles, CA 90031

Hornall Anderson Design Works
1008 Western, Suite 600
Seattle, WA 98104

Independent Project Press
PO Box 1033
Sedona, AZ 86339-1033

Justintime Dimensional Greeting Cards
P.O. Box H
Newtown Square, PA 19073

Kolar Design, Inc.
308 East Eighth Street
Cincinnati, OH 45202

Carol Lasky Studio
30 The Fenway, Suite C
Boston, MA 02215

Laughlin/Winkler Inc.
4 Clarendon Street
Boston, MA 02116

Lind Advertising
15 Trask Street
Gloucester, MA 01930

Love Packaging Group
700 East 37th Street North
Wichita, KS 67201

M/W Design
149 Wooster Street
New York, NY 10012

Mammoliti Chan Design
P.O. Box 109
West Brunswick
Victoria Australia 3055

Midnight Oil Studios
51 Melcher Street
Boston, MA 02210

Mires Design, Inc.
2345 Kettner Blvd.
San Diego, CA 92101

Modern Dog
601 Valley Street, # 309
Seattle, WA 98109

Stewart Monderer Design, Inc.
10 Thacher Street, Suite 112
Boston, MA 02113

Muller & Company
4739 Belleview
Kansas City, MO 64112

New Idea Design, Inc.
3702 South 16th Street
Omaha, NE 68107

Mark Oldach Design
3525 North Oakley Blvd.
Chicago, IL 60618

Platinum Design, Inc.
14 West 23rd Street
New York, NY 10010

Puccinelli Design
116 East de la Guerra Street #2
Santa Barbara, CA 93101

Mike Quon Design Office
568 Broadway, #703
New York, NY 10012

Jeff Reynolds Design
820 Zimmerman Lane
Santa Rosa, CA 95409

Rickabaugh Graphics
384 West Johnstown Road
Gahanna, OH 43230

Heather Robinet
1230 Virginia Avenue, NE, #2
Atlanta, GA 30306

Javier Romero Design Group
9 West 19th Street, Suite 5
New York, NY 10011

S&N Design
121 North 8th Street
Manhattan, KS 66502

Beth Santos Design
2 Village Hill Lane
Natick, MA 01760

Sayles Graphic Design
308 Eighth Street
Des Moines, Iowa 50309

Schmeltz + Warren
74 Sheffield Road
Columbus, OH 43214

Shimokochi/Reeves
4465 Wilshire Blvd., #100
Los Angeles, CA 90010

Sibley/Peteet Design, Inc.
965 Slocum
Dallas, TX 75207

Siebert Design Associates
1600 Sycamore Street
Cincinnati, OH 45210

Smullen Design
85 North Raymond, Suite 280
Pasadena, CA 91103

Sommese Design
481 Glenn Road
State College, PA 16803

Michael Stanard, Inc.
1000 Main Street
Evanston, IL 60202

Studio MD
1512 Alaskan Way
Seattle, WA 98101

SullivanPerkins
2811 McKinney, Suite 320, LB111
Dallas, Texas 75204

Supon Design Group, Inc.
1000 Connecticut Avenue, NW, #415
Washington, DC 20036

Julia Tam Design
2216 Via La Brea
Palos Verdes, CA 90274

Tilka Design
1422 West Lake Street
Suite 314
Minneapolis, MN 55408

Vaughn Wedeen Creative
407 Rio Grande NW
Albuquerque, NM 87104

Watts Design, Inc.
444 North Wells Street
Suite 204
Chicago, IL 60610

WCVB TV Design
5 TV Place
Needham, MA 02194

WS Design
409 Locust Street
Sausalito, CA 44965

WYD Design, Inc.
61 Wilton Road
Westport, CT 06880

Index